You Are There

You Are There

Restoring Churches, People, and Places

ROBERT W. CAMPBELL

Foreword by Ken Wytsma

Illustrated by Caleb Campbell and Meg Campbell

CASCADE *Books* · Eugene, Oregon

YOU ARE THERE
Restoring Churches, People, and Places

Copyright © 2016 Robert W. Campbell. All rights reserved. Except for brief quotations in critical publications or reviews, no part of this book may be reproduced in any manner without prior written permission from the publisher. Write: Permissions, Wipf and Stock Publishers, 199 W. 8th Ave., Suite 3, Eugene, OR 97401.

Cascade Books
An Imprint of Wipf and Stock Publishers
199 W. 8th Ave., Suite 3
Eugene, OR 97401

www.wipfandstock.com

PAPERBACK ISBN 13: 978-1-4982-2101-6
HARDCOVER ISBN 13: 978-1-4982-2103-0

Cataloguing-in-Publication data:

Campbell, Robert W.

You are there : restoring churches, people, and places / Robert W. Campbell.

xvi + 128 pp. ; 23 cm. Includes bibliographical references.

ISBN: 978-1-4982-2101-6 (paperback) | ISBN: 978-1-4982-2103-0 (hardback)

1. Human ecology—Religious aspects—Christianity. 2. Human ecology—United States. 3. Environmental protection—Religious aspects—Christianity. I. Title.

BT 695.5 C30 2016

Manufactured in the U.S.A. 04/07/2016

Scripture quotations taken from the New American Standard Bible®, Copyright © 1960, 1962, 1963, 1968, 1971, 1972, 1973, 1975, 1977, 1995 by The Lockman Foundation. Used by permission. (www.Lockman.org).

Scripture references marked Green Bible are from the New Revised Standard Version Bible © 1989, Division of Christian Education of the National Council of Churches of Christ in the USA. Used by permission. All rights reserved.

Scripture quotations marked NLT are taken from the *Holy Bible*, New Living Translation, copyright ©1996, 2004, 2007, 2013 by Tyndale House Foundation. Used by permission of Tyndale House Publishers, Inc., Carol Stream, Illinois 60188. All rights reserved.

Contents

Foreword by Ken Wytsma | vii
Acknowledgments | ix
Introduction | xiii

Chapter 1
The Cute Little Nightmare | 1

God sends people to places

Chapter 2
And a Train Runs Through It | 13

Chapter 3
You Are the Bread and the Wine | 25

God sends people to restore places

Chapter 4
I Walk in My Garden in the Cool of the Day | 41

Chapter 5
Going to Seed | 53

God restores people

Chapter 6
Manure is Compost, Not Fertilizer | 67

Chapter 7
The Root of the Problem | 77

Chapter 8
Redeeming and Recycling | 88

Chapter 9
Just Plant Onions | 99

God's restored people restore people and places
Chapter 10
You Are There | 113

Appendix | 125

Bibliography | 127

Foreword
by Ken Wytsma

I met Robert Campbell at about the same time that the Lord began to deal with me about some of the bad theology of creation that still holds sway in much of the evangelical church. That was at an A Rocha weekend retreat in the hill country of Texas, where I heard Peter and Miranda Harris (A Rocha's founders) and Eugene Peterson lay out a more biblical understanding of our relationship to God's good creation. Robert, who pastors a church in California, was one of a large room full from people of all walks of life who were passionate about their Lord, about his kingdom, and about justice, but most of whom had a much better understanding than I about how our attitude toward creation plays into our discipleship.

Creation belongs to God. It also belongs to us for our health and well-being. Additionally, per Scripture, we owe a service to creation as stewards. Our sense of justice and our sense of what we owe to others must include an accurate theology of creation and creation care.

As I travel and speak on justice, one of the characteristic mistakes I try to correct is the idea that justice is a cause, an adventure, or simply an issue to take on. Sure, sex trafficking in Asia matters deeply, but if justice corresponds to what ought to be, then it *also* matters how I treat my wife, how I respond to the person who cuts me off on the road, and, most certainly, how I relate to God's creation. We aren't simply called to do certain acts of justice. We are called to become just.

Justice is a right relationship with God, self, others, and creation. Creation is an inextricable part of life and the matrix of relationships in which

Foreword

we find ourselves. Creation is tied to justice and human flourishing and creation is tied, when abused, to injustice and suffering.

The poor live downstream and downwind of environmental degradation. The lives of the affluent are largely insulated from air and water pollution, but these things affect the poor directly. And my use of consumables says something directly about whether I see myself as more important than others in this world.

It isn't easy—it certainly isn't for me—but the biblical demand for justice requires a holistic view of goodness and equity in this world, not a compartmentalized one. And when we talk holistically, we must necessarily address our relationship to where we live, to the communities we inhabit, and to the soil, water, air, and living things that were there before us. Wherever God places us, as persons who care about justice, we should endeavor to make our place flourish like a well-watered garden—both metaphorically and actually.

You Are There offers a message that all followers of Christ, pastors and laypeople, need to hear—that we who are redeemed are called to bring redemption to the places we live, all the way down to the dirt. Robert Campbell is highly qualified to deliver this message, since he has wrestled with it and lived it out—in his personal life, his family, his church, and his larger community.

This is not the sort of call to care for the environment that you might expect. It doesn't attempt to provoke guilt or anger. Rather, it talks hopefully and matter-of-factly about appreciating God's handiwork, learning from creation, and leaning into the natural seasons, all as part of what it means to be a follower of Christ. Robert delivers this message in a style that is personal, personable, and filled with personalities—those of his flock and neighborhood. You'll get ecology, gardening, justice, human nature, food and wine, and a whole lot of theological wisdom, all of it in easily digested stories and down-to-earth reflections that come directly from a grounded life both lived and examined.

You'll also get an introduction to A Rocha, the Christian conservation organization working in twenty different countries. And you'll receive practical and simple ideas for how you, your family, and your church might live more justly in relation to creation and more faithfully honor Christ, who is both Creator and Redeemer.

I'm happy to recommend this important contribution to a necessary conversation.

Acknowledgments

How do you begin to give thanks to those people who have shaped your life for the forty-five years that have prepared you to take up pen and paper? Many more thanks are needed than many be possible, or at least reasonable to write down. If you are not mentioned by name, please know that I am more grateful than I could ever say for the way you lead me, follow me, and walk with me.

> Thank you to the people and place of Santa Margarita
> for changing me.

It is not easy for a town, especially a small town, to accept a new pastor. You have welcomed me with more grace than I could have ever deserved, thank you. You have taught me how to live here with you. You have given me opportunities to lead committees and fundraising groups. You have allowed me to join in your good work that makes this town a better place and the people a better people.

Thank you to my friends, too many to name, in the Santa Margarita Gateway Committee, Santa Margarita Lions Club, and the Santa Margarita Senior Citizen's Club (though I am not technically old enough to be a member). Thank you to the SLO Sheriff's Activities League for venturing out on a new program. Thank you to those who have taught me how to live in this place with its native grasses, wildflowers, oak trees, creeks, and cattle. Thank you to the neighbors on K Street in particular. You have made this little corner of the world a wonderful place to belong. More importantly, each and every one of you have made me better for knowing you.

Acknowledgments

Thank you to Santa Margarita Community Church for growing me.

You had a gracious vision for serving your community already in place when I joined you in this ministry. And you have not slowed down one day since I've known you. You are gracious with your time and generous with your money. I doubt anyone but me knows how amazing you really are and how much you really give and serve. Thank you for allowing me to walk with you. Thank you for hearing me out on creation care and for giving me time to pursue speaking and writing with A Rocha. Thank you for throwing your all behind Creation Care Camps; the whole world is being blessed by you.

To the staff—Andrew, Karin, Lauren, Carrie, and Bob—and elders: thank you for being just screwed up enough to be gracious. You know how important that is to me. Because you have seen your own sinfulness, you have given up on expecting perfection, even of your pastor. I am grateful every day that you give me permission to be wrong today if that is what it takes for me to grow in Christ tomorrow. You have put together much of what was broken in me.

Thank you to A Rocha for putting the pieces together for me.

I always wondered how dirt and Jesus would come together in my life, and you at A Rocha have made it happen. From that first introduction by David and Ashlee, we have been wholehearted friends and missionaries seeking to restore people and places. Tom and Maria, thanks for extending your family to include me and mine. Peter and Miranda, thanks for the leadership and community that you have provided, especially for graciously remembering and inquiring about how we are doing since we last met. To the board and staff, all of you, thanks. Every day with you is a joy. This work with you restores my soul.

Thank you to my family for living it with me.

To my parents and siblings, thanks for never letting me settle for the time and place where life found me. Thanks for giving me the encouragement to keep going and thanks for always welcoming me home.

To Julie, Caleb, and Meg; you live this life with me, and I would not have it any other way. You are the people who have always restored me

Acknowledgments

in whatever place I have been. The sky over our back fence would not be as blue without you. The chickens would just be birds without you. There wouldn't be half the joy in blackberries without you to pick them, eat them, and share a tart sherbet with me. I enjoy this Santa Margarita life with you; every horse show, service project, church service, and school event—even the yard work, most of the time. Thanks for going to seed here with me. May God cause us to grow in this native soil, to flourish as he created us to flourish, and may he keep putting people and place back together through us until that one day when he restores all things in the new heavens and new earth.

Introduction

The local church is the best way to restore people and their places. That is, God restores people in local churches and those churches are there to restore both their local people and their local place. It is the work of each and every church in each and every location to heal the real brokenness that has been taking place between people and their environment. The local church is God's program, and the good that he desires to see done in the world starts there. Jesus is building his church and the gates of hell will not stand against it, neither will wars or rumors of wars, climate change or rumors of climate change. He founded it, commissioned it, presently empowers and guarantees its success in the Great Commission and the great commandment. The good news of Jesus' life, death, and resurrection transforms people and transformed people transform places. The church is God's way of getting his restored and transformed people in the right place for dominion that is redemptive in this fallen world, for putting people and place back together through preaching the gospel and by serving in Christ-like love.

This book is an encouragement to every local church to fall in love again with the "local" part of who we are and all that it entails, especially the limitations of a particular people and a particular place. This is a pastoral conversation to help put the church back in its place, literally, not figuratively. People and places will be restored when local churches make local disciples who follow Jesus all the way down to the dirt.

A Pastoral Conversation

I'm a pastor of the old school. That means that an ordination vow has been exacted over my life for the spiritual growth of one local congregation, one

Introduction

particular body of the people of God in a particular place. I pray for them daily, by name, and they pray for me. I speak the Word of God to them, week after week, and they speak it to me. The one thing on my mind on any given day is how the gospel of Jesus Christ might aid one or two of these men and women to take one more step towards Christian maturity, one more step on the journey towards holiness. For me, this is a very personal calling. I love them. I ache for them. I do not run a church; I pastor a people.

And I pastor a particular people in a particular town. Not a spectacular people in a spectacular town, but I think both they and it are the best in the world.

Every Sunday morning I stand behind a pulpit at 9 AM and 10:45 AM and I look at my people, the people I live with and play with between Sundays. At that moment, when I first step onto the platform and turn towards them, I see them as if I've never seen them before. I see the church of Jesus Christ, called out from the world, kept by their Savior, a holy nation, a people for God's own possession. I see them as the holy congregation that they are, all the while that I know what the prior week was like for most of them. This one's daughter has struggled, and it has been tragically hard on the woman and her husband. That one lost his job without notice and is uncertain how to pay for his kids' college. I see them as they are and my heart leaps within me as our time transforms. "This hour is not like every other hour," we say together and, we add old words like, "Let us worship God." In that sacred hour, God does for us what he promised to do, though it is still so inconceivable to us, he meets us in the open Word, in bread and in cup. He hears our prayers and joins in our songs. I am their pastor; everything that I am is to serve that moment in their lives.

And then comes Monday morning. I return to my study and they return to the classroom, the paddock, the drill press, the science lab, and the business office. But what happens to the holy hour? What happens to the sermon preached? That sermon wasn't just preached to the church but through the church. I preach for them, in order to create conversations that follow in their small groups, at dinner tables and in coffee shops. They then walk the good news preached into every corner of the community while I am home recovering from the sermon. The people and place where we live is better because of them, because they are a placed people. I hope to walk with them until I bury them, one by one, in the Santa Margarita Cemetery, or, if God wills, they bury me.

Introduction

If I cannot do that for you Sunday morning, hopefully someone is, hopefully you have a pastor who is looking out for your spiritual growth. If you do not, stop here, put the book down, and find one. And don't try too hard. If you have a list of criteria that is too long, you will never find one and it is at least partially your fault. You have a list if you are looking for a service club, but not if you are looking for a people to love and to grow with. Eugene Peterson has given the advice to find the closest small church within walking distance and learn to love the sinners there.

I think becoming part of a church would take about a year. You've got three categories of things to work on in order to make it succeed. First, you need to work on yourself and keep working on yourself the whole time—keep learning, keep growing, keep yourself motivated because it will all pay off in the long run. Second, work on finding a church that actually opens the Bible on Sunday morning. I don't mean they put a verse up on the screen or tell you a nice story. That preacher's story is not the inspired Word of God that the Spirit will use to change your life. You've got to value Bible teaching enough to look past whether the preacher is old or young, in a tie or in jeans. Then, third, patiently get involved. You are not there to revolutionize the place. Humbly attend regularly. Go to study groups, attend prayer meetings, help clean. Render whatever service you can offer while the church learns who you are. Settle down; make friends with the intention of keeping them for life. If we all took responsibility for our own growth and our own involvement in the church, it would be a much better experience for everyone and it would more honestly reflect the kind of mature and loving church community that Jesus had in mind when he created the church with his gospel.

Let me be a pastor to you for a few pages, as if we were sitting down for a cup of tea at The Porch, or whatever your local coffee shop is called. Perhaps you could grab a group of friends from your church to read along with you and discuss what you are reading.

Where to from here?

The local church is best suited to put people and place back together, which is what we mean by creation care. God sends people to places, particularly, God sends people to restore places. He starts with restoring people and then, God's restored people restore people and places.

Introduction

First, *God sends people to places.* God has sent the local church to both a particular people and a particular place with a gospel mission. He sends individuals who are restored by the good news of Jesus Christ and they gather together to organize for the supernatural work of restoring those people and that place.

Next, *God sends people to restore places.* God owns the place where you live and has plans for its restoration. You were sent there to be part of that plan. Sometimes we act as if God created the world and then handed it over to us to use as we see fit. Biblically speaking, God still owns the rights to the universe, he never gives up his own dominion. Our dominion is always under his dominion.

Third, *God restores people.* The difference between what God created us to be and do and what we actually are and do is what is wrong with our world. That is, the problem is localized within our hearts even before it is systemic and worldwide. God's first work of both social and ecological restoration is restoring our hearts through redeeming grace that comes by faith in Jesus Christ as Savior.

Finally, *God's restored people restore people and places.* The people restored by the gospel, saved from sin by the Savior, are prepared, placed, and organized to join in the work of restoration. God's people are in the business of both redemption and recycling, putting people and place back together. God's people restoring people, through great commission preaching, and places, through great commandment loving, are what we call a local church.

People and place come together in the local church

As a churchman, I don't often know where I fit in the conservation movement, even the Christian conservation movement. I read stories like *Under the Bright Wings*, about the founding of A Rocha International, and *Planted*, about A Rocha Canada, and find myself both inspired and just a little jealous. Yet, I will never live that life. I will never live in or lead an environmental study center from a Christian perspective. What am I as an ordinary Christian supposed to be doing in this presently troubled world? Do I recycle? Reuse my grocery bags? Is it enough to live "simply"? What does it mean to live simply anyway?

How are local churches to be involved in creation care? In the USA it is hard to even bring up the conversation without getting into a political fight.

Introduction

Is there just another program to run, another package to buy? We churches and especially church leaders tire of someone else trying to sell us another program. Are we simply the funding source for the next parachurch NGO who thinks we are not doing a good enough job at something else? That is how it comes across when outside Christian groups seek to engage the local church, and that is part of the reason it hasn't gone well.

Through my involvement with A Rocha, a Christian conservation organization, I find myself in the middle of heated conversations between the evangelical church and those with environmental concern. It is not uncommon for the church to take quite a beating for not being there when the creatures they were given dominion over needed them most. Some of the criticism is called for; some is certainly not. It has been said that the primary cause for the destruction of the environment is the biblical concept of dominion. It is far more likely that the damage comes from the exercise of human dominion as if it were outside of the dominion of God who created all things. This puts it back on the shoulders of those who live in God's world without bowing to him. Specifically, nonbelievers or shallow disciples.

Local church engagement may not solve every ecological problem in the world, but it will make a profound and immediate difference. It will lead us to abandon big environmental theory, which is easy to fight about because it is impersonal, in order to take up the simple act of caring for real people who live in a real place. We may still fight with our neighbors about our own backyards, but even the fighting will be different when it is face to face. A Rocha Founder Peter Harris often speaks of the overlap between the world's biodiversity hotspots with large concentrations of Christian churches. Former A Rocha USA Director Tom Rowley gets even more specific, pointing out that when using seven measures to map regions of biodiversity importance, Christians are the dominant faith group in all seven regions. If the local church could catch this simple vision of the need and responsibility to care for creation as vitality connected to caring for the people, we would change the world.

Rather than beat up "the church" as an organization, whose primary God-given task is making disciples, this book hopes to help put the local church back together with its place. The simple, commonsense reality is that you cannot love people and destroy their place and you cannot love a place and ignore the people who live, work, and worship there. Read along and I will tell the story of the place and the people that have helped put

Introduction

me back together, the people that live in the place called Santa Margarita, California.

Come and see my people and my place through the pages of this book. Come follow Jesus with us, all the way down to the dirt.

Chapter 1

The Cute Little Nightmare

"This whole town could fit in my church!"

That is how I reacted to my first visit to Santa Margarita. It's nearly true. The town is home to 1,259 residents within the village reserve, 1 elementary school, and 2 churches—1 Catholic, 1 Protestant. The church I came from could comfortably seat 1,000 on a Sunday in a brand-new facility. The old Community Church building in Santa Margarita could fit on its platform, three times over.

Was this where I was to be the pastor? Was I to lead the people of God in this place?

As my wife Julie and I drove from suburban Southern California into town for the first time to meet the committee who was seeking a new pastor, we were both excited and terrified. We were excited about the new possibilities for us, for our family, and for the work of God that we might take part in. We were terrified because all the people we knew and loved were behind us. The people who knew us, loved us, who noticed in our eyes when something was wrong and left flowers on our doorstep just to say, "I love you."

Every pastor goes through this experience, at least once in their ministry lifetime, and it is as awkward as it sounds. Think a blind date, but with a hundred people at one time. Think going to bed with Rachel after a night of celebrating only to wake up next to Leah! Sound like fun? Actually, it sounds impossible, but that's the way we do it. The Evangelical Free Church of America, the denomination that has meant so much to us for over twenty years, has a "placement process" that matches churches looking for a pastor with pastors looking, or at least willing to consider, a new church ministry. When the Free Church "Yenta" asked to take Julie and me for coffee, we knew what that meant. Dennis knew us, loved us, and took such a personal concern for our family that when he said, "I think you need to look at Santa Margarita," that we listened.

We drove into town, and then right out of town before we even knew we had arrived. You've heard stories about towns so small you'd miss them if you blinked, and it's true. Santa Margarita has one exit off Interstate 101 without another off-ramp for five miles in either direction. It's either Exit 211 or it's nothing. This was not quite what we expected. I had met the previous pastor, who faithfully served this church and town for nearly seventeen years. He told me stories of the place that had me envisioning some mix between the Mitford of Jan Karon novels and a Eugene Peterson book. At first I thought, "He lied!" A few years later, I'm convinced he was toning it down to not incite any pastoral jealousy in a brother.

That first visit didn't actually go very well. First visits often don't. The time with the people was amazing; the time with the place was difficult. Dave, the smiling, soft-spoken committee chairman, met us with a warm welcome and prayed for us. Dave always prayed for us. During that time in life we talked and met with several churches about serving as their pastor and only Dave prayed for us, with us, out loud, every time we talked. Dave prayed with us and then drove to our first visit in his blue diesel Volkswagen Jetta, just the three of us.

Now, a seasoned rural minister had warned me that every small church has a power broker in it. So, I figured this is it. Who else would be the first visit? Pulling into the driveway of the simple little bungalow, built to house railroad workers at the turn of the century, we could see an older woman sitting in the corner window that I have since learned she sits in

The Cute Little Nightmare

nearly every day, reading the newspaper and keeping watch over her town. We entered through a side door without knocking—the suburban dweller inside of me was already uncomfortable with this. When we got inside, ninety-year-old Miss Hazel was playing the piano with her back to us, playing like only a seasoned professional could do. Julie stopped, grabbed my arm, and choked back some tears. The blue carpet, paneled walls, and gray hair at the piano felt like walking into her Nana's house. Actually, we were walking into the house of the town grandma. If this was the power broker, we could learn to love her.

On the first night in town with the search committee members and their spouses we ate barbecue hamburgers, played a game of Apples to Apples, and told stories about our lives. I don't remember if anyone drank wine, but in a wine region it seems to be par for the course. The formal questions and interviews followed later, but it all began like this: good people, enjoying each other. Those few days with the pastoral search committee were wonderful, absolutely wonderful. I could have stayed right there, laughing with these new friends, forever.

It was the smallness of the town and especially the smallness of the church that caused the terror in us. On a full day, the old split-level church could seat ninety-three if you folded the people in carefully. We affectionately named it "the cute little nightmare." It was an amazingly cute, small-town chapel, but was insufficient for the day's ministry and was approaching need of repair. The county government would not permit improvements without opening up the door to expensive modern retrofitting.

We walked down the turning and leaning staircase where the children gathered in rooms with bare concrete floors because, in a wet year, water could seep up through the concrete and flood the nursery. Jokes about how often the story of Noah had been told in that church seemed to be carefully scripted to go along with the tour, though we were assured that it never lasted for 150 days and that no soul had been lost yet. We could picture our young children, in a basement, singing Veggie Tales songs about Noah in hip waders. We returned home more than a little discouraged, not knowing how these people and this place would go together for us.

The debrief with our friends and counselors was difficult. We couldn't quite translate our experience.

"That's the church!" one of our friends exclaimed with not a little laughter as we showed off the pictures of our trip.

"Yep, there's the front . . . and there's the back, you're looking at the whole darn thing." I said in response, feeling somewhat defensive of this people and place that I had only just met.

"But you teach more people than that in a Bible study," another added, suggesting that maybe this move would not be the right direction on the ladder. At that kind of moment, friends must find it difficult to not become Job's counselors. If they say, "looks like a great opportunity," then we would be leaving them.

A couple of wise counselors for us, who were themselves not quite at home in suburbia, spoke with a different tone. "Looks like a community that could fit you well, Robert," they said. And that got us thinking.

Maybe the trouble was actually inside of us. Maybe this church was really a healthy body looking to raise up a new generation of Christians in that place. Maybe our experience was blinding us to something wonderful. Small church had been a bad experience for us in the past. Small church meant long hours and late phone calls. Small church meant high expectations and low pay. Small church meant the 20 percent of the people who do 80 percent of the work is actually under 20 people. For us, small church had meant exhaustion, underappreciation, personal failure, guilt, and outright pain. But did that mean it was true for this church?

Now began the long process of discerning with God the difference between our fear and reality. We didn't put out any fleeces, since sheep are not readily available in suburbia. We'd probably use a goat now; every neighbor has a goat or two for weeding. Personally, I've never considered Gideon an example to follow. I would never want to encourage anyone to disobey a few times before obeying. I can imagine God saying, "You've got until the count of three." This was more about examining our hearts. We needed to seek guidance in asking some difficult questions: What part of our fearful response has to do with Margarita and what part is our own past? What is something to go back to them and talk about? Is it appropriate to go and honestly ask, "Is one hundred people a good core or a dying church?" Can we ask about the absence of a youth program? How well have children done who grew up in this church? Can we ask more about the history of the people in the church, so we can learn their stories and feel the stability of three and four generations serving in one place? That is what we decided to do. We went back and asked a million questions, mixed in among times to play, eat, and laugh, which you just have to do in a place like this.

The Cute Little Nightmare

In this way, the people and place of Santa Margarita had already began to help the Campbell family grow in our walk with Jesus long before we arrived in town. They pushed us to set aside our fear and to trust Jesus. They invited us to walk with them and give up the control that comes from fear and risk a little bit on a people and a place in God's great reconciliation program, the local church. The lessons they have taught me about restoring people continue everyday. There is something small town people know about Christian living on a human scale that most of us don't. By scale, I mean that size, numerically or geographically, at which caring for people and place becomes inevitably impersonal, unneighborly. There is something that Christian ranchers know about a daily, absolutely true walk with Jesus that happens with actual people in an actual place. Their faith is lived out in the dirt that they nurture and the animals they feed. There is something about the people of God that I have only really understood after living in this parish. I have learned, hands on, the biblical truth that people and place always go together.

People Are for Places

God has always combined people and place. It has never been otherwise and cannot possibly be otherwise. In Genesis 1 and 2, God creates mankind, male and female, and places them in a garden. The garden was a real place with a real name. It was memorable for its gold and precious stones and was bound by the flow of four named rivers. God put the man and woman there *to work* it or *to cultivate* it, that is, *to serve* it and *take care* of it. The word translated *serve* in the Genesis passage is also used in Exodus 3:12 to describe the Levitical service to God in the tabernacle. The term for *take care* shows up again in Genesis 30:31, describing the way one shepherds the flocks, and in 28:15 protecting people who need it. God put people in the place to do his will there, to carry out his instructions.

God planted the seeds and Adam and Eve were supposed to work to bring the flowers. He created animals for the ground, birds for the sky, and the man and the woman were responsible for it, to act towards it as God would act if he were living there himself. If all things went as planned, there would be more glory in the garden because Adam and Eve were in it. They were a people in a place.

In Genesis 12, God chose Abram out of the land of Ur, where his father lived, and brought him to a place where he and his descendants would be the source of blessing to all the families of the earth. Abram became Abraham, the father of a nation of people still tied to their land over three and a half millennia later. God's people and God's place go together.

In Psalm 104, the author sings about the greatness of God's act of creation. God separates the waters in order to form a place.

> He established the earth upon its foundations,
> So that it will not totter forever and ever.
> You covered it with the deep as with a garment;
> The waters were standing above the mountains.
> At Your rebuke they fled,
> At the sound of Your thunder they hurried away.
> The mountains rose; the valleys sank down
> To the place which You established for them.

The psalmist then describes the divine interconnection that happens between the people and the place. God channels the water to cause grass to grow; grass feeds the cows, and humanity eats the cows. It becomes this happy, ingenious cycle of people and place as God intended. In the same Psalm, God waters the grapes; grapes become wine, and wine makes man's heart glad. The psalm ends with us, the readers, joining in the song of creation. God has always put people and place together.

One morning, a local cattle manager named Jeff came to talk with our children. We had hiked them out on a local trail to see and touch what the psalmist was talking about. We arrived at our designated space under a magnificent coastal live oak and sat down in the dirt quietly. The cows were in another paddock so the only sounds were the wind blowing through the perfect California grass and, of course, the noise of twenty excited children who were, literally, as loud as a herd of grazing cattle. Then a dust cloud rose up over the hill, bringing an old ranch truck along with it. Out of the truck stepped a real cowboy. Yep, Wranglers, pearl snaps, dirty boots, and a hat. These were country kids, so a real cowboy probably impressed me more than it did them.

"We rotate the cows onto this paddock every few months," he said. "The time for rest is just as important for the grass as the time for the cattle to eat it down."

"Why is that?" asked one of the children, Malachi, who was now sitting so close to the cattleman that he could probably smell the manure on his boots.

"Because the grasses grow healthier after the cows eat them down. And then the cows come back to eat the healthier grass and become healthier cows."

"Why?" another child asked again.

"Because God made the black cows, who eat green grass that we can't eat and turn it into white milk and red meat that we can," said the cowboy, in true Psalm 104 fashion.

And when a cowboy speaks words like that, the preacher just gets out of the way. People and place, grass and cows, go together.

It's not just in the Old Testament either. Paul, in giving his definitive apologetic sermon on Mars Hill, explains how God has both determined our appointed times and the boundaries of our habitation when he said,

> He made from one man every nation of mankind to live on all the face of the earth, having determined their appointed times and the boundaries of their habitation (Acts 17:26).

All the way at the far end of the Bible, in Revelation 21, God will create a new heaven and a new earth where he will dwell forever with his people.

> And I heard a loud voice from the throne, saying, "Behold, the tabernacle of God is among men, and He will dwell among them, and they shall be His people, and God Himself will be among them."

That is, he will create a new place for his new people. And those who are not his people will have a new place too, but you do not want to go there. God's people are never without a place—a good place.

Places Are for People

I found myself reading the book of Revelation in a time of drought in California, an apocalyptic drought. The drought continues to this day; we will be looking for the sun to turn black like sackcloth next. The front lawn died sometime in November. We still hold a small memorial in its honor every Monday and Thursday when we have permission to run the sprinklers, but choose not to. It is dead, all of it, from that bit full of iris gone wild to the hollyhocks along the drive and down into the swale that borders every property in this small town. It is dead and looks like it won't be coming back.

Restrictions are in place, gardens are withering, and the well level record shows a little lower every week.

> Average annual rainfall: 26.0 inches.
> Three-year average annual: 14.1 inches.
> Supply status: Alert

Neighbors are literally borrowing water from neighbors, hauling it over to wash dishes and brush their teeth. Park rangers walk the shore of what used to be a reservoir, now 24/7 and even 4 percent full . . . which means 76, 93, and 96 percent empty, dry, providing next to nothing for myself, my family, and my quarter million neighbors in the county.

We passed frightening in March, right after a freak storm gave us half of the years' rainfall overnight. We passed frightening, did not slow down for awful, and are now looking devastating in the face. And his face is looking a bit chapped already.

Everyday our local paper laments the slow growing disaster with Davidic tones, "How long O Lord?" The waters that bounded this Edenic paradise have long since ceased flowing. But one day the water of life, in the new heaven and new earth, will bring healing to the nations.

I could not help but notice that wonderful imagery of Revelation's "one day" when all things are made right. On that day, there will no longer be any curse. On that day, there will no longer be any night. On that day . . .

> There will be a river of the water of life, clear as crystal, coming from the throne of God and of the Lamb, in the middle of its street. On either side of the river was the tree of life, bearing twelve kinds of fruit, yielding its fruit every month; and the leaves of the tree were for the healing of the nations (Rev 22:1–2).

On that day, God will use water as he has always intended water to be used. Water will serve the healing of the nations. That is what God desires for the water that once flowed through my town, the water I used to grow annual grass where perennial grass flourishes natively. I think maybe the drought has taught us something. It seems that those neighbors are now using water in a more biblical sense when they truck it next door as an act of love, for the healing of nations, or at least the healing of neighbors. They are putting people and place back together.

People and Place Always Go Together

Many false dichotomies have risen up in the world that separate people and place, some have even worked their way into the church. But from the first

The Cute Little Nightmare

garden to the last one in the new heavens and new earth, people and place always go together.

What does it mean that people and place go together? It means that you cannot actually ever separate the two. You have a place you live in and it cannot be otherwise. Everyone you know lives in some place and every place you know is home to some people. If you mistreat it you are being inconsistent with your Christian faith and are specifically damaging some neighbor who depends on it. That is not to suggest that you have to be involved in policy or politics, though you can be and some need to be. Creation care is a call to be more fully Christian, to think about the actual daily effects of your Christian faith on all of your thoughts and actions.

You are some place. You live, love, play, and work in some *place*. You worship and evangelize some place. That is how all things began and how they continue . . . for you and me and everyone. There is no such thing as a people without a place. The people you love, they are some place; the people you do not love, they are some place. The people God wants you to evangelize, they are some place. When we want to reach a people with the gospel, we send missionaries to that place. Lost people have a place. What I'm trying to say is that people and place go together, are created to go together.

Call it "the healing of the nations," or shalom or restoration or redemptive dominion. Whatever you call it, these are just a few examples, but enough to see that God created people and place to go together and that he has sent his people, the church, to get organized with the gospel message to every place as stewards, as servants, acting toward that people and place as God would act if he were standing there himself. Let me say it again, you can't separate the two—people and place always go together

God sends people to places

God has sent the local church to both a particular people and a particular place with a gospel mission. He sends individuals who are restored by the good news of Jesus Christ and gather together to organize for the supernatural work of restoring those people and that place.

Chapter 2

And a Train Runs Through It

"Sorry we were late, we got stuck behind a train at the crossing."

Sounds like a poor excuse for the chronically tardy, but it makes sense in Santa Margarita. We all use it because it's so often true. One is as likely to get stuck behind a train as he is to find the crossing gates up and the lights off. Southern Pacific Railroad tracks bisect the town. As you travel north through San Luis Obispo the engines slow down and work a little harder as they wind and climb their way through the tunnels and over the Cuesta Grade. You descend through a magnificent oak-studded pass and emerge, with a great bend, into our little town. Just out of the right side windows as you come out of the woods are the old corrals, still standing and still in use for over a century, thanks to cowboy craftsmanship. Neighbors will wave to you as you cross Wilhelmina and Bill's On Track Studio, but the only sounds you're likely to hear are the piercing horn reminding locals to keep a safe distance and the *chuga-chuga* of the train on the

God sends people to places

tracks. That's the sound of Santa Margarita, the sound of home. On the left, notice the glorious backsides of the lumber yard, diesel repair, feed store, The Range, and others before running right alongside the community park where children nearly fall off their swings when the horn sounds. During the summer movies in the park, the movie will pause so the kids can run to the fence to wave as the train goes by. It's not like the movie can continue with all that noise anyway. With a great curve to the northwest, crossing the old highway, you say goodbye to town for a while. But do keep looking out the left-side window where the old *assistencia* stands like a monument tying this place to its people.

They have provided only three available track crossings for our people; that first one at Wilhelmina, another at Encina, and the last where Estrada meets Highway 58 at the far end of town. Old-timers tell of the days when the train stopped at the Santa Margarita Station. They tell of when the engineers would block all three crossings at once, leaving the poor south side residents locked in until lunch time was over or the engine was repaired. There is only one way around, but that would take you nearly an hour out of your way. Children would spend the night in the apartment above the station with the family who lived there and hang out the old mailbag in the morning. The best story is about the corpse car that would come through. Back in the days before the highway, which was before the freeway, I Street was the main thoroughfare. You could find the church, the constable, a few general stores, a blacksmith, and a mortician. A "corpse car" would come through on the train to pick up or drop off for the mortuary, and in those days the bodies were all packed in ice. Ice was a rare commodity before refrigeration. Town children would gather excitedly and the mortician would let them take some ice out of the car to make ice cream. What can you say? It was an old western town with a train running through it. The train defines our place; we are a railroad town. You wouldn't visit Santa Margarita without seeing the trains or at least the train history displayed at the Southern Station.

Its significant places or sights define every locale. New York City has the Statue of Liberty. Philadelphia has the Liberty Bell, though it has a big crack in it. They should probably tell you that ahead of time—truth in advertising. Paris has the Eiffel Tower. Rome has the Colosseum, but don't scratch your name in it; a Russian tourist was fined over 20,000 euros and given a five month suspended jail sentence. Washington DC has the Founding Farmers restaurant with its gourmet popcorn, and a few other buildings you may find significant, but I can't remember why. To be there is to be part of that place. To live there is to be defined by those points of interest.

Your Placed Life

God has sent his people, transformed by the gospel, into every place on the planet. This is step one in putting people and place together, by putting people with God's heart in those places. God intends a placed life for us, one that lives on the earth as much as in heaven. One that cares for and enjoys this creation even as it awaits the new creation. In fact, it is in part through you that God is bringing the fruit of redemption to creation, making it new. Together is whole, that is how God created both us and all things. Sin has broken heaven and earth apart, but God is putting them back together in Jesus, and he has given us that same ministry of reconciliation. Until the day when it is final, creation groans for you to be whole; the people long for a peacemaker, and the place longs for your cultivation. God has given us this task of dominion that is redemptive.

But "the world" is a big place. And I have trouble just finding my way around the rural areas that make up my parish on the Central Coast of California. *Where does Route 229 lead again? Will that dirt road over Pine Mountain really take me to Pozo?* To even think about the mission of God in the world can be overwhelming. And it isn't just the scale; it's the scope. We are called to preach the gospel to the ends of the earth. Now add feeding the poor and looking after orphans and widows. The needs are endless. To add caring for creation makes it all but impossible—we may as well give up. We have only so much time, energy, and money. Besides, what difference can our little actions make? And even if they can make a difference, which actions do we take?

I get it. We feel paralyzed.

But, what if God has intentionally put us in our place for his worldwide mission? What if we focused on the dirt we walk on—the place where we live, work, worship, and play? What if we just focused on the place God put us? The place matters tremendously. That place where you live, with its train, statue, tower, bell, or restaurant. Eugene Peterson writes of Christians as placed people in his book *Christ Plays in Ten Thousand Places:*

> Everything that the creator God does in forming us as humans is done in place. It follows from this that since we are his creatures and can hardly escape the conditions of our making, for us

God sends people to places

everything that has to do with God is also in place. All living is local; this land, this neighborhood, these trees and streets and houses, this work, these people.

This may seem so obvious that it doesn't need saying. But I have spent an adult lifetime with the assigned task of guiding men and women in living out the Christian faith where they raise their children and work for a living, go fishing and play golf, go to bed and eat their meals, and I know that cultivating a sense of place as the exclusive and irreplaceable setting for following Jesus is mighty difficult.[1]

It is *mighty* difficult.

You have a place. You were *sent* there like any missionary has been sent to a place and its people. God has given you to that place and he has given that place to you. It is a beautiful exchange of gifts. The place gets you and you get the place. That place is to reflect him more fully when you leave than it did when you arrived.

Being Put in My Place

I've always struggled with how people and place go together for Christ followers in a fallen world. But I am learning, growing. Here is how it began to come together for me, though it took a while.

I was born and raised in suburban Southern California. My town of Montclair, not to be confused with Claremont, which registered the name first, was known for the Montclair Plaza, a grand shopping mall that folks traveled from miles around to join the liturgy of the mall: shop, walk around, or just hang out. The Southern California valley at the base of Mount Baldy in the San Bernardino Mountains had been an orange orchard sometime prior to my arrival on the planet. In the 1960s, the citrus was razed and in its place grew up a series of contiguous housing tracts named, as they all are, after the unique kind of nature that used to be there. I lived on Fauna Street, where little fauna actually lived anymore. Suburbia ran in every direction as far as a boy could travel. Both my elementary school and high school were within walking distance, while the middle school took an uphill drive from Mom to get there. But I could skateboard, downhill, all the way home! Mt. Baldy stood like Zion over our town. We boys couldn't wait until we were allowed to ride our bikes up to the dam and then all the way back down.

---

1. Peterson, *Christ Plays in Ten Thousand Places*, 72.

And a Train Runs Through It

As teenagers we would ride our skateboards down the mountain roads at night, but no one was supposed to know about that. It was a good place to be as a boy.

Butch lived directly across from me. He and I played ball in the street. We even painted a baseball diamond on the cul-de-sac asphalt. Sometimes everyone would come out to play, young and old, and those games would last for hours. On the end of the street, just where the curved end touched the busy Monte Vista Boulevard, Mr. Norman's magnolia tree invited endless hours of imaginary boy battles as we "pulled the pins" on the seed pods and threw the prickly ends at each other. And then sometimes we would just smell those flowers, the smell of my childhood. It was to me like the scent of oil coming down on the beard, even Aaron's beard, down upon the collar of his robes. How good and pleasant it is for boys to dwell together in unity.

Luke lived just passed the culvert. We would play now and then, when he was visiting his dad there after his parents divorced. All the way at the top end of the street lived the chicken boy. I never knew his name, but the only time I met him, he sang a chicken song, thus becoming "the chicken boy" in the neighborhood lore of the lower half of Fauna Street. When I was old enough to go up that far, we would start our skateboards in his driveway and ride them, sitting down, all the way home. The old neighborhood was good to me and was stable. Everything else seemed to change around me, but home and neighborhood, my place, stayed the same.

I loved education of all sorts in those days, and I often dreamed that I could have been part of some of the great conversations of the past that changed the world. Old books became my good friends. So my family teased, "Robert, you were born in the wrong time," and I believed them.

I knew that there had to be something more for me and that it required dirt and God, the only two things that made sense in my life. I can still recall the shaping influence that long, filthy Boy Scout hikes had on me. My mind holds snapshots of the snow-covered Graveyard Peaks in California's Sierra Nevada. I can hear the water rushing from beneath the hardened snow in the month of August as it made its way into the Devil's Bathtub. The trail followed one tributary until it broke free into an majestic granite-bounded, high-mountain lake. You could hear the sound of the river long before you saw the water. We boys, who were crazy enough to swim in it, made rafts of old downed trees for epic battles over the small rock island in the middle. Then we would fish with hooks on strings tied to long sticks and make mountain trout our dinner. While it's been thirty years, it feels like yesterday. That is what I see when I read, "The heavens declare the glory of God." The dirt in me heard their sermon and said, "Amen, yes." God put dirt in my soul.

So I studied Environmental Sciences and became a Christian at the university while doing so. It's still an odd story for me to recall how God arranged a meeting with a man who had been a youth pastor and an a great influence on this fatherless boy years earlier. He took me to his desk and showed me his prayer book. There was my name at the top of the list. "I've prayed for you every day for the last five years," he explained to me. I was dumbstruck. While I was wandering far and wide, he had prayed for me every day. He took me in, taught me to study the Bible, and launched me in church ministry. I still didn't yet know how the Bible and creation care would come together for me.

Fast forward to a rainy fall day in Bellingham, Washington, some dozen years later. Perhaps it was just a drizzle, as it does there, but for Southern Californians, it felt like a flood, and we kept looking for Noah and hoping for a rainbow. My wife Julie and I were strolling that amazing little berg while visiting friends and doing some doctoral research at Trinity Western University, just across the US/Canadian border. The day was filled with coffee, as most are in the Pacific Northwest, and used bookstores, as most are for the Campbell family. After stumbling into a conversation on South American literature at the counter of Henderson's Books, Julie looked at me and said, "You weren't born in the wrong time, just the wrong place." My life hasn't been the same since. She was right, and I knew it.

I, like so many of us, allowed the understanding I had of myself to be only theoretical. That is, my identity was based on an idea, but without grounding in anything real; no actual dirt and no actual people. I was the guy "from another time" and I lived how I thought that character would live. Julie put my feet on the ground. Julie tied my sense of self to the place where I lived and walked. From then on I began to look at my place as a part of me. But what would this look like in my real, day-to-day life?

I went home to Corona, California, where I served as the Pastor of Outreach and Community for a joyous group of Christians who love Jesus and their community in amazing ways, and I still love them dearly. Corona is a thriving suburban metropolis in California's Inland Empire. For you who live outside of California, go to Disneyland and drive straight east for about half an hour and you're there. The Circle City, as it's known, took its nickname from an auto race that ran on the circular Grand Avenue in 1913, 1914, and 1916. That round road shaped the people and the place of Corona. Not many years ago Corona had been a small community outside of the great Orange County development, originally planted with acres and acres of lemons. Yet, when housing boomed in the 1990s it spilled over and kept going as individuals were willing to commute farther and farther on a busy freeway to get to work. A town of 30,000 became home to more than 150,000 before you could blink. Neighborhoods exploded, schools exploded, and churches exploded.

I returned from Bellingham with my eyes open, asking myself, "What does it mean to be in this place, this specific location, this geography, and this environment, as a missionary sent by God?" God answered with a lesson by happy accident when I offered to bring volunteers to an event favored by the mayor. Karen was a kind and active woman who truly made the town a better place. This was a simple little carnival promoting drug awareness among our 56,000 students in the school district. Red Ribbon Week, they called it. While this didn't fall into our "mission" per se, it was a service we could provide and I was ready to learn to be more fully where God had put me. The field at a local school was set up like a carnival and students who took part in the Red Ribbon Week got an invite to an afternoon of play. Well, we showed up, about fifty of us, and just did odds and ends for the event day, nothing spectacular. We made cotton candy until we were more covered in sugar than the paper cones being handed out. We chased footballs over and over and over again as contestants lined up to throw them through a spinning tire. For some reason, this game was the hit of the day. It was still going even after all the rest were torn down and put away.

The event was not particularly better because of us. The earth did not shake. Heaven did not open. No kids put their faith in Jesus because we handed out tracts with the cotton candy. But my relationship with those very people of my community changed that day because I, and the church, took interest in what mattered to them in a tangible way. The carnival was their program and we participated. From then on the mayor would hug me whenever we met up. She showed me how to be a part of the community, the actual place and the people who lived there. I don't know that I had realized that I wasn't a part before that, but *I wasn't* a part before that. I, and the church, were on the outside looking in, as if the people were not our people, just people to be reached. It was like the place wasn't our place, just where our tract home happened to be. We became a people who cared about the place where God had put us and it was the mayor who taught us, or at least she taught me and I taught the church. Do you see? The very same thing that you and I do all the time, volunteering, became an act of love for a very real someone in a very real place. I was now doing it *for them* and not just because it was the right thing to do. I'm not sure I would have seen that occasion if I had not had my eyes opened to my people and my place that day in front of Henderson's. I would not have been the blessing to them or received the blessing from them.

That was the day I was converted. I became a parish pastor. God put people and place back together for me. *Those* people in *that* place. And it was not long before serving them forced me to honestly look at the way that the local reservoirs in Lake Matthews and Lake Perris affected their health and happiness. Or the way the chemical plant in the hills above impacted the air they breathed. We cannot love the people and ignore the place they live in or steward the place without loving the people.

Many of you are like me, living lives that are full of good ideas about beauty, right in the midst of beautiful people and a beautiful place that you seldom notice. Others are very aware of the beautiful people and are serving them humbly in the name of Jesus, but have not even noticed the birds and the trees, the water and the frogs. I am urging you, with all my heart, to let God put people and place back together for you. The two always go together.

Being Sent to a Place and Its People

It wasn't long after these ideas began to take root in our hearts that God sent our family to the ends of the earth. He moved Julie, Caleb, Meg, and me to Santa Margarita, an eclectic, historic western town on the Central Coast of California. If you have never been to California, you may not know that there is a Central Coast. If you do, you may have expectations of what it is like. Most folks I meet when I travel envision Los Angeles or San Francisco when they think about California, or maybe Hollywood. It's all artificial concrete places and artificial plastic people. That is true in many places north and south of us, but now wedge in an open coastal region, as green as Ireland in the spring, and sprawling with agriculture instead of suburban housing tracks. That's the Central Coast, exactly halfway between Los Angeles and San Francisco.

And a Train Runs Through It

Santa Margarita is a unique little town because it is entirely surrounded by one of the oldest and longest continually working cattle ranches in California. The Santa Margarita Ranch was originally formed when Mexican Governor Manuel Jimeno granted 17,734 acres to 26-year-old Joaquin Estrada on September 27, 1841. Don Estrada was famous for his hospitality. His Days of the Dons celebration, which commemorated Mexico's independence, could last for weeks, with rodeos, races, and barbecues. During those days, cowboys and vaqueros would herd their cattle from the surrounding ranches into Santa Margarita to be put on the train going north to feed hungry gold rushers. The young men would spend their hard-earned monies in the saloon before ending up in the old concrete jailhouse that still stands just down the hill from the community church.

The old ranch house barn was built long before Estrada showed up. California Mission fathers traveled along the El Camino Real, setting up mission parishes to reach out to both Spanish and native populations. Missions were usually built about a day's journey apart. One sits in San Luis Obispo, about ten miles south, and another in San Miguel, twice that to the north. An *assistencia*, or mission extension, grew up in Santa Margarita, providing cells for traveling priests to stay the night, a chapel for Mass, and a stable for their animals because the trip north from San Luis Obispo crossed an arduous pass. That *assistencia*, one of the oldest stone and mortar buildings in California, is the defining building of our town. It's pitched roof and stone walls feel sacred; they feel like they hold more memories than mortar. A few years ago, we restored worship to that old building after over a century by gathering there to celebrate the resurrection on Easter morning, which we now do every year with a growing number of community members.

The Union Pacific railroad travelled south from San Francisco and stopped in Santa Margarita. From there, the stagecoach carried passengers over the Cuesta Grade, past the 8 mile house, to pick up the train again in San Luis Obispo headed for Los Angeles. It was decades before the two connected. In 1889, Patrick Murphy, second owner of the Queen of the Ranchos, made a deal with the railroad to auction off 320 acres of 25-by-150-foot lots for railroad workers, creating the town of Santa Margarita. The fiesta that accompanied the auction was one for the record books with barbecues like only an old western cattle ranch could host. One hundred and two lots were sold the first day, and the streets were named in the old-fashioned way, alphabetically, and with the cross streets named for

God sends people to places

Murphy's favorite nieces: Wilhelmina, Maud, Maria, and Helena. The town boundary has not grown by one inch since that auction day over 120 years ago. And a train still runs through it.

The town has filled in with houses and families; some original families continue five or more generations on. We had an era not unlike Radiator Springs, the fictitious town from the movie *Cars*, when Highway 58 was the primary east-west route from the coast to Bakersfield, and we've settled into a semi-rural bedroom community with the perfect mix of the political Left and Right, ranchers and hippies, Chevys and Volvos.

God sent us here to serve this people and this place. I love this town. I was made for this town and it took me thirty-eight years to get here. This is my place. I am "the town pastor," even to those who are not a part of the church. Here, I am learning, day by day, how people and place go together. It is here in Santa Margarita that I am learning much about the way place defines people, people define place (for good or for ill) and how God reunites dust and breath to make us whole again. It is here where I first encountered the work of A Rocha and that twenty-year-old question of how my pastoral work and environmental concern go together is finally being answered. David and Ashlee, members of our community church who were already involved in the conservation work of A Rocha, took a summer sermon I preached, on Psalm 104 again, one of my favorites as you can tell, and sent it to the good folks at A Rocha. I later received an invite to speak at an A Rocha symposium on the topic of why the church should care about conservation. I accepted the invitation on the condition that I could speak about why the local church should care about conservation, that is how believing that we are sent as missionaries to a place shapes the way we live in that place as people. When I arrived to speak, I browsed the book table and noticed *The Green Bible*, and I have a beef with *The Green Bible*.

Did you know there was a *Green Bible*? I don't mean "green" in color, but "green" in perspective. That is, an environmentally friendly, ecologically responsible Bible. It is printed on recycled material and all the biblical passages which emphasize creation care are printed in green, kind of like how the old King James printed the words of Jesus in red. "With over 1,000 references to the earth in the Bible, compared to 490 references to heaven and 530 references to love, the Bible carries a powerful message for the earth."

I am a "green" Christian by their description. I believe that when God created men and women in his image, he instilled in us the responsibility to act as he would act towards his creation. It is his creation and we are his stewards. I believe that Christians cannot be responsible to the biblical great commission to evangelize and disciple people if we ignore the place where they live. In fact, I believe that a Christian cannot love people without loving the place where those people live. I live a life that seeks to exercise personal stewardship for both the people and the place God has sent me. My neighbor eats and drinks water; my care for those is love for him. So, know that my beef with *The Green Bible* has nothing to do with environmental responsibility.

On the other side of things, my beef with *The Green Bible* is not that it could possibly imply that there is neutrality between Christian creation care and pagan environmental activists. Non-Christians approach the subject with their own religious presuppositions, such as the Sierra Club, which endorses *The Green Bible*. *The Green Bible* demonstrates common ground, but that must not be misconstrued as neutrality. It is a thoroughly Christian work.

My real beef is with the cows in *The Green Bible*. Here is what I mean. As already mentioned, in Psalm 104, God causes the rain to fall on the mountains. God carves the beds of streams that lead the waters from the mountains to the plains where it waters the grasses for cows to eat . . . and people eat the cows. It is a beautiful divinely ordered picture of creation in which we are reminded of something forgotten in our day: cows eat grass, which we cannot eat, and from it produce milk and meat, which we can eat.

So, what is the problem? It lies in where the green letters turn black. Nearly the entire psalm is printed in green letters, as it should be. But the there is this one black verse in the midst of sea of green. The black verse, 23, reads this way: "People go out to their work, and to their labor until the evening."

Really? First of all, if the poem is about stewardship, then the whole poem is about stewardship. Secondly, do people and their work not fit into "passages that speak to God's care for creation"? Cows, water, and grass are part of God's care for creation, but people and work are not?

A biblical view of creation care includes humanity, living under the rule of God, working hard so that both people and place are better and more clearly reflect God after our use. We are stewards, not owners. Psalm 104:23 should be in a darker green! A biblical ecology hinges on the way that people work the land they actually live on. People and place go together, and the good work of men and women, sent there by God, blesses both people and place. So, I added my beef with *The Green Bible* into my talk that day. *The Green Bible* itself is a very good thing, but I couldn't pass up the chance to talk about people and place, cows and humanity together, especially in a way that allowed the tongue to be firmly planted in the cheek. They laughed, took it humorously as intended—and then gave me a copy of the *The Green Bible*. And I still serve with A Rocha today. The last laugh was theirs.

God sent you to that place

Your community is your place—the place where God has sent you. Your place has a story within the story of God. Your people have a history within the history of the gospel. Think about that. When God planned, before the foundations of the earth, to put the pieces broken by sin back together, he had you and your place in mind. When Jesus lived a righteous life and died a sacrificial death, he already had strategy for getting that good word to your place. On the day he commissioned his disciples to declare the good news that he had conquered sin and death, and that through faith in him, you and I could be freed from the guilt and consequences of our sin and live new lives, the whole and blessed lives we were created to live, on that day the story included you, your place, and your people. It took nearly 2,000 years for the gospel of Jesus to reach your town at the ends of the earth, but it finally did and now is in your hands. God sent you as missionaries to both the people you live with and the place you live in. Praise God that you are there. You are God's people in that place, whether a train, a river, or a freeway runs through it.

Chapter 3

You Are the Bread and the Wine

US Poet Laureate Emeritus Billy Collins tells of finding a romantic poem, written by a struggling poet, printed in an airline magazine, stuffed into a seat back pocket. The poem began with great promise:

> You are the bread and the knife
> The crystal goblet and the wine...

He graciously accepted the task of rewriting the poem as it should have been written, and his efforts resulted in one fantastically funny piece of verse more about himself than the beloved. After the ups and downs of love and lambasting, "Litany" concludes:

> I am also the moon in the trees
> and the blind woman's tea cup.
> But don't worry, I'm not the bread and knife.
> You are still the bread and the knife,
> you will always be the bread and the knife,

God sends people to places

not to mention the crystal goblet and—somehow—the wine.[1]

I can't help but hear "you are the bread and wine," when I read this poem, even though I know full well what it says. It must be the churchman in me. The divinely inspired act of eating around a common table, feeding each other, as well as the stranger, and especially breaking bread together in church community is the humble context in which God brings people and place together, putting his people in his place.

Heidi works with Peg at Studio Uproar, the center of the art universe in Santa Margarita, the sun that all things artistic orbit around. The two of them never fail to bring smiles and joy, not to mention beauty to our people and our place. I will take the long route home on a Monday morning walk from the coffee shop, just to see if they are in the study to stop and chat for a while. They are my people. They make this town a better place by being who they are. Peg works in multimedia, paints and textiles mostly, in a terrifically irreverent way. She lives outside of town, but we still call it Margarita. Heidi lives in town, down where the road dead-ends into the creek. (In a small town, the first question you ask someone you meet is, "Where do you live? . . . Oh, you mean next to so-and-so.") Heidi's primary discipline is ceramics. She forms these magnificent, earthy pieces that are somehow useful and beautiful at the same time. I often think God must have had her "useful bowls" in mind when he created clay on the third day. We commissioned her to create communion utensils for our little country church. We talked in detail about the designs, grapevines on the goblets and wheat on the plate.

"Do you want this or that?" she asked, seeking to provide exactly what I had it mind. She seemed anxious to make sure that I would not be disappointed. We walked around the studio together, picking up pieces and discussing options, light or dark, glazed or unfinished.

"Here are pictures of mugs I made for Chris and his new wife." She displayed photos of these two amazing mugs with Greek words about love carved into them. Chris had just graduated bible college and had gotten married.

"I want you to make it, you're the artist, I love your work, I want your ideas," I responded. And she did just that. She took her wheel and threw two ceramic goblets, handcrafted with love, in our town, for our worship to hold the fruit of the vine and across the top it reads, "I am the vine." Also,

---

1. Collins, *Nine Horses*, 69.

there was one square plate, unfinished brown and glazed beige, intricately designed with wheat and the words "I am the bread." This sacred plate holds bread, also made by hand, from which we each break a portion to eat because we are one body, one local church, in this place.

There is a growing contingent of people who have abandoned the local church. They say things like, "I am spiritual but not religious," or "I don't need a church to worship God," or "I have the best pastors to listen to at home online." A second group travels miles to go to a church outside of their place because they like the programs, or they like the personality of the pastor. They haven't abandoned *the church*, just the local part of it. Others say that they are part of the global "church," but not part of a local church, which really has no meaning at all. In fact, there is a theological term for someone claiming to be part of the "church" but not the local church; it's called a "Cop Out." That usually serves to keep any kind of authority at bay, so I reserve the right to take off at the first sign of discomfort. But it's often the discomfort that helps us grow, and it is in staying put that we can make a difference. A church, to be experienced, is always and only local.

The purpose of this chapter is to move the conversation from the individual *you* to the communal *you* of the local church, the body of believers that you belong to by default, if not by practice.

I understand that many have had a difficult, painful, and even abusive relationship with the local church. Church and I have not gotten along very well. Yes, I am a pastor. But as a paid church member or a regular member, I always seem to come out on the short end of things. At first, I determined that the problem was the people, so I began a personal revolution to demand that people change. I insisted that those who lived in my circles, or those unfortunate enough to run into me, knew when they were hypocrites or when their self-centered American lifestyles were destroying the planet and inflicting unjust suffering on the third-world slaves who sewed their big box store clothes so they could save forty-seven cents. The revolution failed; all that happened was that no one wanted to be around me. I realized that people are just people, inside or outside the church.

The problem, it seemed, was with the institution of the church, organized religion, which is kind of a funny phrase. What is the alternative? Disorganized religion? Usually that means I want to make up my own way. So I began a personal revolution to create a level playing field within the church. I spoke to church leaders as if they were buddies. "Hey, Jack, how's it going?" I wrote articles for the church newsletter to rally all to the side of

God sends people to places

equality. No leaders! We all are servants under Jesus. That failed too when I learned enough to know I was wrong, and the church really does need leaders. There is such a thing as biblical leadership. Some men and women do abuse their power and run the church like their own little fiefdom and treat themselves like kings and queens, but the problem is with those people, not the church. I'm glad that I have met and sat under leaders who did not abuse their power but used it for others.

When I came to realize that the only common factor in each situation was me, I began a personal revolution to grow up in Christ and be a mature part of the church . . . that one is still in progress.

I learned to love the local church while in seminary. Each year during commencement, the first and second year students would become a tremendous choir singing to the graduates, launching them out into ministry. We would sing "A Mighty Fortress is Our God" and a hymn I had never heard before that time, " I Love Your Kingdom, Lord." It goes:

> I love Your church, O God
> Her walls before You stand
> Dear as the apple of Your eye,
> And held within Your hand.[2]

And so I learned to love the local church. Actually I learned to love a facsimile, a theory of the local church. When I got out into the real world, I found out . . . that those songs about the church are just an earlier version of Photoshop. It is dirtier, it is uglier, and it is messier than you ever realize looking at the textbooks or hymnals.

Organizing transformed people

The real church, if we boil it down to simplest definition, is a local gathering of believers. It's a gathering of people defined by their faith in Jesus and the dirt they walk on. The local church is God's way of getting his people in the right place for the job. The church that always exists in some actual place in some actual time—Corinth in 50 AD or Santa Margarita in 2014 AD—is best suited to exercise a redemptive dominion where we live. The church is God's program, and it is always local.

You, church, are the local gathering of believers in your place. Your hearts have been renewed by faith. You are now defined both by your faith

---

2. Bock, ed., *Hymns for the Family of God,* 545.

in Jesus and the *dirt* you walk on. Do you remember Paul's opening line in 1 Corinthians: "To the church of God *which is at Corinth*"? Or how about to the churches of Galatia or Thessalonica or Laodicea or . . . you get the point. God established a church there as a base of equipping workers for the gospel task. This is the supernatural reality of the local church. God is now active in that place through your life and ministry. God has placed a church to organize restored people for the work of restoration.

The strength of the local church in my community is its mission to its place and the people of that place over generations. Santa Margarita Community Church started over sixty years ago when Grandma Hazel and a group of ladies decided that the children of Santa Margarita needed a Sunday School. It began in Hazel's living room, moved later to Proud's garage, and finally to the newly built church on the hill, sometime before 1960. A powerful earthquake hit the Central Coast back in 1993, causing major damage and some loss of life when a few old masonry buildings came tumbling down. The local government implemented retrofitting on all unreinforced structures in the county, including our own. When they came to shut us down, Grandma Hazel, then over seventy, said, "No, there is rebar in those walls, I tied it myself." That same old church is overrun with children every Sunday. The church that started as a local rural village mission is still a local mission today. It started in Grandma Hazel's living room, and we buried her with her husband Andy just last week. She died just days shy of her ninety-fifth birthday. Hazel's wishes were to be buried in the cheapest pine box; "Don't make a fuss," she said. But we made such a fuss. We made a fuss worthy of a woman who spent over sixty years of her life putting people and place back together through the gospel of Jesus Christ.

The way local mission works out for us is by simply being part of the community: David and Ashlee starting an A Rocha project here; Su serving in our local government where she participates in the bureaucratic and environmental conversations as a Christian woman; it looks like the church joining in with Samadhi, Heidi, and Jen for the community-wide cleanup day; like Jeff and Lindsay running a fine local restaurant, buying the food they serve from local farms and dairies; and it includes many in the congregation participating in local Community Supported Agriculture. It's just normal, everyday participation that makes us a local church, bringing people and place together. That is what we are trying to do. We are not taking over, we are participating and bringing the most good we can bring.

God sends people to places

Our greatest impact will always be with the people we live among and on the dirt we walk on every single day. These are our people; this is our dirt.

The point I'm making is that the local church is God's way of getting his people in the right place, restored people to restore people and places. Santa Margarita is that place for me. After 20 years of struggling to connect theology and environmental studies, God is making me whole again . . . and he is doing it here, with my toes in this dirt, with this dirt in my body through the vegetables, the cattle, the water, and the wine.

I make bread as a hobby; sometimes it is more than a hobby. I mean, I am a little obsessed with the idea, the preparation, process, and especially the taste of bread. Actually, I think I have a gluten-free intolerance. It was a school chaplain who first turned me on to it. He told a story in chapel one day about how making bread slows him down in the midst of all the mental chaos that university study brings with it. I needed some slowing down, so I made my first loaf and set it to rise under a tree in the yard of our very first married place, a little grandma suite on a hillside with a view. The bread overproofed in warm sun and was a total failure. But it didn't stop me from baking and wasn't the last failure. Julie sent me to a bread-making class at a local cooking school, just so someone could put my hands on a batch of dough and say, "This is what it is supposed to feel like," and I've never looked back.

Sourdough is the holy grail of bread in my opinion, and my family has always agreed. Our then–ten-month-old son sat with us for three hours at a dinner table eating San Francisco sourdough bread during my sister's wedding rehearsal dinner. Every time he got fussy, we just tossed him another piece and all was right with the world. Sourdough somehow lines up heaven and earth. I am sure there was sourdough in the garden of Eden. And yet, any attempt I made at sourdough bread failed over and over again. One Sunday I had grand plans to make matzo bread for the communion service. It turned out beautiful on Saturday night. Handing the bread to the preparers, I went about my Sunday morning routine and on into the service, and then it was time for communion. We read from the Scriptures, "On the night he was betrayed, he took bread . . ." and we handed out the bread. After a prayer I spoke the words to my people, "Take and eat it, all of you, feed on him in you hearts by faith with thanksgiving." And they ate. At least they chewed . . . and chewed . . . and chewed. That bread was like rubber in my mouth. I was supposed to speak again after the bread, but I couldn't get it down. More than that, I was supposed to speak blessings, and

You Are the Bread and the Wine

all I could think about was cursing the preparers for not telling me the bread was inedible! I swallowed hard and went on without looking anyone in the face, and I gave up on sourdough, too, for over a decade, until recently.

My friend Bethany gave me a bit of starter that she had been nurturing for a few years, and I've slowly turned it into Santa Margarita sourdough, more affectionately known as #margaritasourdough. Sourdough is bread made by the long fermentation of wheat flour and water. It takes on the bacteria and yeast of the locality in which it lives. When I feed my sourdough starter with water from the minera-rich town well, it is literally Santa Margarita sourdough. We are actually consuming a little bit of Santa Margarita whenever we eat it. The town is becoming a physical part of us more and more every day.

The same is true for the local wine. The Paso Robles Appellation runs throughout much of northern San Luis County and produces many award-winning wines. You may find them on your shelves labeled "California Central Coast" or "Paso Robles." Over my back fence, on that old Santa Margarita Ranch, are approximately 930 acres of magnificent grapes, laid out by the legendary Mondavi family for Ancient Peaks Vineyards. Being the good neighbors that we are, we support this local business and our friends who own and run it. They wisely take advantage of the unique terroir to create bottles of fermented magic. The terroir is the specific geography, geology, and climate of the place that creates a taste that cannot be duplicated anywhere else in the world. One such place in the AP vineyard is known as "Oyster Ridge," due to the giant fossilized oysters shells that quite literally push up out of the soil on that hilltop. Coastal fog pours over the Cuesta Pass, just fourteen miles from the Pacific Ocean, like waves that came in with just a little too much force. It slides and drips down over the ridge causing the warm daytime temperatures to drop dramatically and the grape sugars to spike. Little pocket microclimates are common for our region. Frost often settles on one part of town while entirely passing over another, just a block away. The wine that bears the Oyster Ridge name stands out for the rich mineral taste and fine tannins that make it a star on our local tables. When we drink that wine, we are drinking Santa Margarita. The place becomes a part of us as much as we are a part of it.

Here is what I'm getting at: you are the bread and the wine of your place. Do you hear the biblical hints in that statement? That is, God has put the place in you and you in the place. The place meets God through you and God meets the place through you in the local church. That is where restoration happens. I am trying to put you in your place . . . and you are going to thank me for it.

Own it and give thanks

Let me be pastoral for a moment. Let me remind you of who you are before we consider what you might do with this deeper understanding of yourself as a placed church. You are Christians, people who have put your faith in Jesus as Creator of the Earth Son of God, Savior of Sinners and Redeemer of all Creation

You are the children of God. You are the church, which Jesus has purchased with his own blood. You are a holy priesthood, a holy nation, a people of God's own possession. You are the sheep of the Good Shepherd, the Bride of Christ, and the body of which he is the head. You are fullness of him who fills everything in every way. You are the church filled with the Spirit of God, empowered for all God's holy work in the world. You are the people sent to serve the garden and preach the good news to all creation—people, plants, and animals. *That* is who lives in that place. Own it, it's yours.

Sometimes we forget who we are and we also forget who Jesus is—thinking him only our personal Savior and not Creator and Redeemer of all creation. And sometimes we forget where we are—in a place, created by God and subjected to groaning with the fall of humanity into sin. When we forget those things, we function on the outer edges of the community and run short reconnaissance missions for evangelism, but we don't really become a part of the community and we don't broaden our care to the larger creation.

In one community in which I served, our church purposefully chose not to have a float in the community Fourth of July parade that ran down Main Street in front of a crowd of happy neighbors. It was one of those classic parades that featured school choirs on trailer beds singing their hearts out even though no one could hear them over the diesel engines, and karate schools kicking and *kiah*-ing their way down the street until they looked so exhausted that you wanted to carry them the rest of the way. Every year someone would ask, "Why don't we have a church float in the parade?" I would point out the members of our church on nearly every float that went by. Dave and his son were on the Boy Scout float. John sat in on the Library Foundation float, and so on. "We were in the parade," I would respond, "just not in a way that demonstrates we were separate. We were actually involved."

Later, I was speaking with a group from a church plant who told me, excitedly, about how they set up a booth at the side of their local 10k run to hand out water bottles with their name on it. I said, sarcastically (I did know them well enough to be playfully sarcastic), "What a great way to show you are not part of the community." If we are part of the community, we will be running in the race, serving on the planning committee, helping to clean up afterwards. We would work, play, and live alongside the people that God has sent us to rather than act as a separate group dropping in a fishing line.

Are you a part of your community? Do the folks in your community think you are a part? Do they want you to be involved? Does someone call you or your church when things are happening? Does the natural world around show your handprints of care or only your footprints of use, to borrow a phrase from Tri Robinson's very helpful book, *Small Footprint, Big Handprint: How to Live Simply and Love Extravagantly*. Let me encourage you to be friends, to serve, to get involved so that your life, your church, and the future good of your place—all of it—are all interconnected. Own it and give thanks.

Of course, that can be difficult, the church and community will not always see eye to eye on some issues.

Environmental issues are hot and personal in any place. In Santa Margarita, it's even more so. Any attempt to develop, build on, plant, or alter the historic cattle ranch that surrounds our community will immediately affect everyone. As local Christian people we must be involved in those conversations, but carefully, doing our best to love our neighbors as ourselves and to encourage others to do the same. The place involved is our place. The water is our water. The view is our view, too. The people involved are our people. Our children go to school together. We laugh together at the summer movies in the park. We love both the people and the place dearly.

The first time we showed an A Rocha promotional video in Santa Margarita Community Church, the only part some folks noticed was Sir Ghillean Prance making mention of climate change in the context of very specifically talking about how the climate where he lived had actually changed over the recent decades. That opened up an intensely personal and political discussion in our small town church, which needed to take place because we love one another. We needed to wrestle together until we got to a common understanding that what we were talking about regarding the church and creation care was not political and could not be dismissed that easily. This is not a political conversation; it is a human one and a spiritual one. A human one in that most poverty and disease is directly exacerbated by environmental concerns and spiritual because the species lost are the handiwork of God.

In his popular book on the western diet, *The Omnivore's Dilemma*, Michael Pollan has a great quote from an old agricultural text:

> Farming is not adapted to large scale operations because of the following reasons: Farming is concerned with plants and animals that live, grow and die.[3]

The church is like that too. It thrives locally because we are concerned with people, plants, and animals that live, grow, and die. Our churches live, grow, and die along with us. We are concerned with the real people and the place where we are sent. Christians can only be personally involved locally. Local is always personal.

Name it and enjoy

Our community participates in A Rocha's Creation Care Camp program where we teach the children these very same principles. Creation Care Camp is made up of four week-long day camps for elementary school children that promote transformational engagement with both their people and their place, which will raise them to follow Jesus all the way down to the dirt. These children are healthier; their place is healthier and their faith is distinctly healthier because of Creation Care Camp.

In the year one curriculum our campers explored and discovered the particulars of their place. What are the particular animals, birds, bugs, and plants God placed them alongside? To do this, we opened up Genesis 2 and talked about the garden God made, which had a name, and the people he placed there, who also had names. We then hiked the children down the very hot road to Matt and Su's several acre gardens on the outside corner of town. That garden provides tomatoes, melons, peppers, corn, and more for friends and neighbors who might want to come by and fill a basket. Sunday morning worship during harvest time in Santa Margarita looks like a farmer's market.

3. Pollan, *The Omnivore's Dilemma*, 213–14.

That sunny California summer day had crossed 100 degrees and we could feel it. We led red-faced children into the middle of the open field with great clods of soil turned up by the tractor plow. They melted with sweat while the windmill stood motionless, without even a breeze to help out.

"Bugs in the garden are both good and bad," said our local entomologist. "Some help the plants and others eat the plants. Go find some and we'll talk about them when you get back."

With that, we set them free with bug catchers, water, and hats on their hot little heads. In the garden, they touched the fruits and veggies, ate the dirt, saw the bees pollinating the plants, and then enjoyed the produce of that garden that grows in the place where we live, the dirt we walk on. You should have seen the looks on their faces when they finally began to notice the bugs. Mimi and Keaden glowed with excitement, and sweat, when they hauled that squash beetle back to the adults standing in the shade of the storage shed.

"That one eats the squash. Look underneath the fruit where you found it, you will see little white trails dug into the gourd itself." So they did, again and again.

"How do you stop them?" they asked, now feeling protective of the garden.

"Well, there are poisons that would do it. What do you think of that?" she asked.

"Why would you put poison on your food?" they shrieked, not even wanting to touch it anymore.

"The other option is to pick them off by hand." This helped put some things in perspective for our little ones; nothing is cut and dry, otherwise the choice would be easy. This was a real garden; this was their garden.

At the end of the day, back in the cool air-conditioned church building, we read the story of Jesus in the garden of Gethsemane and then about the garden in the New Heavens and New Earth. It is more than a children's story to learn that what began in a real garden will end in a real garden city. It is the good news of all good news that while Adam disobeyed in the first garden, Jesus obeyed perfectly in the second, so we could live forever with him in the third. This is the dirty gospel. It is easy to get from dirt to Jesus because he does it all the time in his own stories.

God sends people to places

That neighborhood garden is now the visual in our children's minds when they read about any of those gardens. It has become real for them. It's like God has moved into their neighborhood, into their garden.

Wendell Berry was certainly thinking about your neighborhood when he wrote:

> The question that must be addressed, therefore, is not how to care for the planet, but how to care for each of the planet's millions of human and natural neighborhoods, each of its millions of small pieces and parcels of land, each one which is in some precious way different from all the others. Our understandable wish to preserve the planet must somehow be reduced to the scale of our competence—that is, to the wish to preserve all of its humble households and neighborhoods.
>
> What can accomplish this reduction? I will say again, without overweening hope but with certainty nonetheless, that only love can do it. Only love can bring intelligence out of the institutions and organizations, where it aggrandizes itself, into the presence of the work that must be done.
>
> Love is never abstract. It does not adhere to the universe or the planet or the nation or the institution or the profession, but to the singular sparrows of the street, the lilies of the field, "the least of these my brethren."[4]

Now we are not just talking about "people," but "neighbors," and not just neighbors but Jason and Brooke, Dave and Lori, Kevin and Edee, Nathan and Cindy. Our neighbors who have shaped us since we moved to this town.

Elsewhere Berry tells about a woman who came up after a lecture and said to him, "I just love the environment." Berry, in his eighty-year-old Kentucky drawl, says he wanted to respond, "You do not. We tend to give things we love proper names."[5] He's right. Names change everything.

At our annual Creek Cleanup Day, we remove all the debris from Yerba Buena Creek, so it won't flood the neighborhood, as it often does. In 1998, the creek was breached, and dozens of neighbors suffered damage when the floodwaters ran down blocks of lettered streets. My good friend Mrs. Dillon lost the back half of her house, which needed to be razed and replaced. She had been in that home for over forty years by that time.

Caleb, Meg, and I were working with Mike in the creek bed and came out next to John and Carol's house. If we did not remove the debris,

---

4. Berry, *What Are People For?*, 200.
5. Berry and Jackson, "The Land, Our Food and Our Responsibility."

it would be their house, their belongings that would be flooded, not just some distant community we see on the news. My son was using trimmers that belonged to Mr. Flynn, so I reminded him of this. He said, "I know that they don't belong to us." But that is not enough. "Not belonging to us" means we don't take them home. "Belong to Mr. Flynn" means giving them back to Mr. Flynn. The name makes all the difference in the world. We are God's people in the right place for the job. So for us it's not just about loving neighbors, it's about loving Dave and Lori. It's about Sarah who benefits from purchasing that cup of tea. It's not just about the environment, it's about Yerba Buena Creek.

Leah Kostamo of A Rocha Canada helped me see the importance of naming when she wrote,

> Learning a name gives worth to the thing named. Think how "unknown" and undervalued you feel when someone can't remember your name. In theological terms naming is the first step in moving from an "I-It" relationship with something or someone to an "I-Thou" relationship, a relationship where a person or creature or even an object becomes known not just for its usefulness, but for its innate worth.[6]

Let me close this with two stories to get you thinking about your place, specifically

Our town is on a common well. The large watershed that flows into Santa Margarita Lake is tapped to pump water from two active wells into two large storage tanks that serve the needs of our people. Just outside of town, however, each family is on their own private well for clean drinking water. Not long ago our local paper ran a story about a man who became seriously ill with an unidentified sickness. It continued to worsen until it was discovered (and I don't know how it was discovered) that a neighbor was dumping his own waste into the sick man's well. Disgusting, I know. It taught me a vital lesson about they way people and place go together and gave me one of my favorite memorable lines about the truth that people and place always go together. Are you ready for it? *You can't love your neighbor and pee in his well at the same time.* Now, you'll never forget it either. You're welcome.

If I couldn't do that to Dave and Nancy, then I shouldn't do it to anyone. Not in Santa Margarita, not in China, not in the Gulf of Mexico. Everywhere is someone's neighborhood.

6. Kostamo, *Planted*, 62.

God sends people to places

A few years ago, while many of these thoughts were still coming together in my mind, I was sitting on a patio on the campus of Trinity Western University in Langley, British Columbia. One of the pastors there said that his church was planning to reach 500 people in the next five years. The request came in response: "Name them." The shock of that phrase brought us to new conversation. Why? We will do things differently when we have actual people in mind. If we are after 500 nameless, faceless people, we will put an ad in the newspaper. If they are friends and neighbors, we will invite them over for dinner.

> *You are the bread and the wine.*
> *You are a local church.*
> *You are God's people,*
> *in the right place for the job.*

You are the local church, an organized group of restored people, on the job of restoring your people and your place. You can know them well. You can know the place's unique glory and specific troubles. You can know your neighbors, their stories, their hopes, and their pains. You can bring the good news of Jesus and the new life that Jesus gave you to them in a way that no one else can. You can know the meadow and the creek and the animals that live in them, as well as the challenges to their survival. You can help. You can put people and place back together. This is the kind of impact that a local church can have that no one else can have because God has sent you there. This is why it is such good news that you are *there*.

God sends people to restore places

God owns the place where you live and has plans for its restoration. You were sent there to be part of that plan. Sometimes we act as if God created the world and then handed it over to us to use as we see fit. Biblically speaking, God still owns the rights to the universe, he never gives up his own dominion. Our dominion is always under his dominion.

Chapter 4

I Walk in My Garden in the Cool of the Day

I walk in my garden in the cool of the day. When my work has been completed, when the sun's long shadows cause everything to appear strangely four dimensional, and the cool ocean breeze is blowing off the coastal range that borders my back fence, I walk out into my garden.

It reminds me daily of that time, however short, when our first parents shared that divine moment with a divine guest. The book of Genesis records the time when God came into the garden to walk with Adam and Eve, clearly implying that this was the daily routine of the three of them together, just like mine. Perhaps it was after a nice supper that they would set out for an evening stroll in the garden where all things were good, where seeds bore fruit after their kind, and where work and worship were united in the real world according to God's intent. Something was different on this night because the man and the woman were different. They had decided that the goodness of the garden with God was not sufficient for their happiness. They had decided that neither God nor his garden was actually good.

They had decided that they would be better than God himself at judging good versus evil. So, on this night, when they heard his footsteps approaching, they hid themselves shamefully among the trees that God created for their joy. Our relationships with God, with ourselves, with each other . . . and all of our walks in the garden have not been the same since.

I walk out into a different garden than that first one. I walk into a garden in a broken world because of that choice of Adam and Eve, which we each then repeat daily. I walk into a garden that is no longer as it was created to be, and I know full well that we are responsible, not God. I walk into a broken garden as a broken man seeking to find God in and among the pathways, the seasons, and the weeds.

Graciously, God continues to walk with his people even after our rejection. It's not the same certainly, but it is true nonetheless. He calls his people to walk according to his commands, to do what he has told us, believing this time that his instruction is both right and good for us. God's commands are like the pathways in my garden that I walk upon. They are not the garden. They bear no fruit, but I could not walk in the garden freely without them. Pathways take discipline to build before you want to walk. Obeying God's commands because I trust God teaches me to walk with him in season and out of season.

When winter arrives in the garden, it limits the garden vegetables to just a few hardy plants that don't sport the vibrant colors of spring plantings, but they are beautiful in a wintery sort of way. This season has already started bringing with it some much-needed rain. My walk will be muddy this evening, even on the pathways. That rain woke up the seeds in the barley hay packed into my garden beds for a warm winter ground cover and quickly turned it into a meadow of flourishing barley grass. The grass is nice but threatening to choke out the real garden. The real garden, isn't that how we think? Winter reminds me that this is the real garden. In some seasons, the real garden has more weeds than fruit, more work than worship, just like the garden of Adam and Eve. In some seasons I cultivate more bugs after their kind than seed-bearing plants after theirs. When I walk in my garden, I have to learn to be content with the season. Winter is a bare season. I have to take time to worship as well as work. Worship sees and values what is there, even in the winter, while work constantly seeks to improve what may not be wrong, just asleep.

Walking with God today has become so much more beautiful because of Jesus. Death and the hard work of the garden is no longer the end of the story. Separation from God, each other, and ourselves no longer needs to be the season that we live in. Now, because Jesus lived a righteous life and died a sacrificial death I can walk into the same broken garden as a new creature myself, learning the seasons and learning to bring worship and work back together. Work and worship meet up when I walk in my garden, people and place, me and my place.

One day God's people will walk with him again in a garden city. Every time I walk in my garden I long for that day. That day when there will be no more slugs and earwigs—or crying, or war, or death. That day when there will be no more weeds—or sin and its painful brokenness. That day when people and place will be reunited as I walk in God's garden, along the paths built for his repentant and restored people at the cost of his Jesus' innocent life. In that season, the river of life will water the garden, the tree of life will yield its fruit in season, and its leaves will be for the healing of the nations. When I walk in my garden, I know that it is just a foretaste of the one that is to come.

East of Eden

If I were to ask you, "Where do you live?" How would you answer me? Would you describe the region? *I live on the Central Coast of California.* Many where I live want to make it clear that we are not in *Southern* California. Would you tell me about the governmental designation? *I live in San Luis Obispo County.* Or would you talk about your street and the neighbors who live there with you? Does thinking this way help you get a better picture of where you are sent by God to bring restoration? Does coloring in the lines help you love it more? Is it beginning to feel more like home? Yes? No? Maybe? What will it take to move you from being displaced to placed as a church? What can move you and me from a separated life into one in which the pieces of place and people are put back together? The same one thing is at the heart of this calling for all of us. It will require that we worship the God who created all things out of the overflow of his eternal goodness and made a home to live in.

I am suggesting that God can best use the church to put people and place back together because he has sent his restored people to a place and organized them for the work of restoration. Now, in this chapter, I want to address your heart towards God and the natural overflow of that heart towards all things God owns. Your response to his ownership of all things will form your ability to be at home there, to live as missionaries in your place. That sense of your place, though east of Eden, will only serve to connect your daily Christian life with the mission of God in the world, which he gave to the local church. Christopher J. H. Wright notes:

> Mission is not ours; mission is God's. Certainly, the mission of God is the prior reality out of which flows any mission that we get involved in. Or, as has been nicely put, it is not so much the case that God has a mission for his church in the world but that God has a church for his mission in the world. Mission was not made for the church; the church was made for mission—God's mission.[1]

The mission is God's mission; the place is God's place. This is a very important starting point.

I live in a church-owned house, called a parsonage. In the mid 1970s Bud Parker led a group of men and women from Santa Margarita Community Church to build a house on a donated piece of property. They purchased and tore down an officer's barracks from Camp Roberts, a World War II military replacement-training center about an hour north, as a source of lumber. Then they put together a fantastic three-bedroom home with a large living room, perfectly fitted for the hospitable kind of life required by a small-town pastor. The quaint house sits on maybe a third of an acre and backs up against the old Santa Margarita Rancho where the fields run on endlessly to the horizon in every direction.

During our initial visit to town, the interim pastor gave us a tour of the house, and we were in love. What a magnificent place! But it was not until the Schliep family came to visit and told us their stories that the house truly became a home. Paul and Sharon lived in the same repurposed house for over sixteen years, raised their kids in it, and left the place far better than they found it. Not that they found it poorly, but they beautified it, made it their own, and added those special pieces that have made a wonderful place to live, even for us. Inside the house, I have thoroughly enjoyed the private built-in study off the garage and the extra space of the bonus room. But the happiness that they left for us to enjoy everyday is on the outside.

"Jon made the gate as a gift to the family," they told us as we opened it to welcome them to our home . . . their home . . . the parsonage.

"I hope he is available to repair it when the time comes." I mention with both admiration that he made the beautiful piece and admission that I could never possibly get it right when the time comes.

1. Wright, *The Mission of God*, 62.

I Walk in My Garden in the Cool of the Day

"We planted the White Alder about twelve years ago." And now it provides plentiful shade throughout the warm summer days as we all lounge underneath it. The canopy shelters a garden party now and then.

Sharon, a master gardener, built and nurtured the most magnificent garden in the backyard. It's been home to both plants and animals over the years. On the right, we walked the circular pathway around herbs and fruit trees. In between run rows of grapes and blackberries, old and well rooted, bearing their fruit in the proper season. This is the garden I walk in the cool of the day, Sharon's garden, a gift to be treasured, an inheritance to be honored.

When we moved in, the church let us paint the house our colors, which means my wife's colors, and cozy it up to fit the Campbells. Since we have lived in the old house, folks from the church have made some significant upgrades, like opening a wall for greater access between the kitchen and the living room. The house has become our home, but it's not really ours and will never be ours. We treat the house like the gift that it is because it does not belong to us. It's our home, but it belongs to our church family. If we respect the owners, we will leave it better than we found it, just like Paul and Sharon. That is what I'm getting at: where you live is home, but you don't own it.

We use the derivative of an old Greek word to describe our place in the world. It is our *ecosystem*. The one who studies it is an *ecologist*, and the one who manages it an *economist*. These terms come across to some of us as scientific and impersonal, but they are really very dear, very intimate, and very biblical. The root of all these is the term *oikos*, meaning house or home. Leah Kostamo again states,

> This is where the definition of "ecology" is helpful: *eco* from the Greek *oikos*, for household, and *logia*, for "the study of." Anyone who has grown up in a household understands that it's a complicated web of interrelated relationships.[2]

Do you hear it now? An ecosystem is a home; it is always somebody's home. If it isn't my home, then perhaps it is your home. Somebody lives on the Gulf Coast damaged by that traumatic oil spill. Are they my neighbors? Are they yours? Place is always somebody's home.

My point? You were sent to where you are, and that place belongs to God; it's his house. Those biodiversity hotspots with large concentrations

---

2. Kostamo, *Planted*, 56–57.

of Christian churches belong to the God they worship. Understanding this makes all the difference in the world, literally. Nothing is "out of sight, out of mind," when God owns it all. "Not in my backyard," is not sufficient advocacy when it is still God's backyard. Now we're stuck. We can't get away from God's house. The whole darn earth is his house, which includes your individual neighborhood, even your backyard. You are renters; you are God's stewards. Whether you treat that house with respect or not will be determined by one thing and one thing only: *do you respect the owner?* Do you worship the God who created all things, owns all things, and intends that the whole created universe serve his pleasure and his purposes all the way down to the dirt?

God created your place

Let's back up a little and get the big picture before we narrow down to talk about your backyard. Where do we start? We always start with God because God starts with God. Have you ever noticed that the Bible doesn't give arguments for the existence of God? This is because God already knows that he exists; we are the ones who lack understanding.

If we start with God, then all that follows will make more sense, will be more beautiful, and will bring about more goodness. Professor D. A. Carson writes that Christians are not suggesting that if you examine the birds of the air or the lilies of the field it will necessarily lead you to faith in God, though it probably should, but that when you start with faith in God it makes the whole of creation more wonderful.

> I am not sure that it is right to argue from . . . the stiffness of the woodpecker's tail feathers . . . to the conclusion that God exists. At the end of the day, God is not merely an inference, the end of an argument, the conclusion after we have cleverly aligned the evidence. But if you begin with this God, the testimony to his greatness in what we see all around us is heart stopping.[3]

Can we care for the environment if we don't start with God? Sure, we can do the actions, but those actions will not flow consistently from what we believe. It will always rub up against our view of the world, and we will know it; we will feel it down deep inside between both ourselves and our place and between our belief and our action. Starting with God makes our

---

3. Carson, *The God Who Was There*, 17.

actions towards our world consistent. Starting with ourselves makes all environmental action somewhat hypocritical. Unless we start the story in the right place, we will always tell the wrong story. Unless we build on the right foundation, the house will fall down. Unless we plant in good soil, the garden will not grow. The story of our world starts with God, who is our one foundation and our healthy soil.

Before the beginning God existed. Our God is the creator of all things, infinitely perfect and eternally existing in three persons: Father, Son, and Holy Spirit. That is how our church statement of faith reads. One summer we taught the statement to our children in catechism form.

> *Question 1: Who is God?*
> *Answer 1: God is the creator of all things, infinitely perfect and eternally existing in three persons: Father, Son, and Holy Spirit.*

A young lady ran into to the Santa Margarita Community Hall, where we were starting to set up for church services, excited to ask me a question. "Pastor Robert," she said, "Keaden has a question to ask you." Her curly haired young cousin came running in behind her across the World War II-era hardwood floors, sending echoes through the empty room. His eyes were wide, and he was out of breath. "Who made God?" Keaden asked, panting with his hands planted on his knees to hold him up.

The last thing I was prepared to do a few minutes before church started was to translate a question of deep theology into the language of a five-year-old. So, I asked him question one of our catechism in response. "Keaden, who is God?"

Confidently, with back straight and eyes bright, he rattled off the answer, "God is the creator of all *fings*, infinitely perfect and eternally existing in three persons: Father, Son, and Holy Spirit."

"So, who made God if God made all things?" I inquired further.

"No one," he declared before bolting out of the room to join the other kids; that seemed to be enough for him.

This is where our story begins, with a truth so simple a five-year-old can understand it and so magnificent it shapes everything that follows.

Our God eternally exists in three persons, Father, Son and Holy Spirit. We start the story with God who was never created; he has no beginning, and he will have no end. God is entirely independent from needing anybody or anything for either his existence or his happiness; God is personal: God has always enjoyed a perfectly personal, fully equal and satisfying relationship in himself. Our God is relational. Way back before anything began

God sends people to restore places

the Father looked at the Son and said, "You are so infinitely perfect," and they were happy. The Son returned the compliment and responded likewise to the Holy Spirit, who is himself the Lord, the giver of life. God has always been happy all by himself, before the beginning.

In the beginning God created all things out of the overflow of his goodness and happiness. That is how it was in the beginning. Everything was good because God is good. Our world, our earth, was good; can you believe it? It was good, and all that existed was happy with God and God with it.

Good is such an important word here. Why? Because God says it so many times; over and over again, the creation is *good* and *very good*. God sees what he has made, and he enjoys it. God sees his world: light and sky, land and sea, and he sees that it accurately reflects his beauty, the eternal beauty that existed before the world was, before even time was. Now you are hearing it, aren't you? Your place, the home where God has sent you was created good and very good. All of your eating, washing, building, gardening, wasting, and polluting—you do it all in God's good house. Stay here a minute; don't rush to the fall. God built a true reflection of himself into the dirt you walk on that it might lead you worship him as the independent creator. Does it lead you to worship him?

As the creator of all that is, God is not a part of his creation. If we drew a line across the entire creation, we would have two categories: (1) On one side of the line, there is God and then (2) on the other side, there is everything else.

This distinction, or separation, between things is an important part of God's creation. It is mentioned no less than seven times in the first chapter of Genesis. And every description of distinction ends by repeating, "It is good."

1. God makes a distinction between himself and everything else when he says, "In the beginning God created all things" . . . and it is good. (Gen 1:1).
2. God makes a distinction between light and darkness when he separates them on the very first day . . . and it is good (Gen 1:4).
3. God makes a distinction between waters above from the waters below and forms the sky . . . and it is good (Gen. 1:7).
4. God makes a distinction between day and night creating days and seasons and years . . . and it is good (Gen 1:14).

5. God makes a distinction between sun and moon, forming a bright light to govern the day and a lesser light for the night . . . and it is good (Gen 1:18).

6. God makes a distinction between mankind and the rest of creation, endowing men and women alone with his divine image . . . and it is good (Gen 1:26).

7. God makes a distinction between male and female, both unique, both image bearing and yet very different . . . and it is very good (Gen 1:27).

This is our starting point; we are creatures among creation, distinct from God and distinct from all the rest of creation as image bearers.

Take the grove of coast live oaks (*Quercus agrifolia*) that congregate the hillside near my home like the oaks of Mamre, just waiting for a divine visitation. Or the valley oak that towers over our house, inspiring praise by declaring the wonders of God as they *pour forth their speech* to all that will hear, as the psalmist writes. Or the downed oak on the new church property that we dream of having Mitch mill into magnificent church doors, inspiring enough that brides will want their photos taken in front of them. How should I feel about them as one who believes in God who created all things? By maintaining a proper distinction between creator and creatures, as Genesis teaches, I am able to avoid two extremes and to settle into a happy and harmonious rhythm in my place.

First, I can avoid the need to raise the tree to a semidivine status in order to give it sufficient value to deserve respect and preservation. I can value that tree because my God created it, and I respect him. Modern environmentalists have an increasingly public problem in that they have no consistent reason to place any value on creation itself, apart from its resourcefulness to people.

On the other hand, I can avoid the mistake of thinking that I am above creation and not part of it. In reality, I am bound to that ancient forest as a fellow creature. The tree is good because it is a tree. It does not gain its value because it has use to me as a natural resource, though it may rightly become a resource at some point. Those trees are fellow creatures, owned by my God. God made those trees, just as God made me. Francis Schaeffer spurred this conversation among evangelicals in the 1960s when he said,

> The tree in the field is to be treated with respect. It is not to be romanticized as the old lady romanticizes her cat . . . . But while we should not romanticize the tree, we must realize that God made

it and it deserves respect because he made it as a tree . . . . The Christian is a man who has a reason for dealing with each created thing on a high level of respect.[4]

In first honoring God as the creator of all things, I also learn to respect his creation. Likewise, I respect the oaks as an act of reverence toward the God who created them. The two are intrinsically tied together.

Your God, who personally exists and personally created all things out of the overflow of his goodness, is very involved with his creation right now in and through you as a local church. He created the place where you live, and he owns the place where you live. And it is very good.

So, while trees and oceans, snowy plovers and kangaroo rats are not equal to God, neither are men and women, boys and girls. We all share a common creatureliness under God. He alone is the creator of all things. This is the world he created and it has a personal story that gives personal worth to all he created. He personally created the place where you live. And he personally sent you to live there to help put people and place back together.

God owns your place

"The earth is the Lord's and the fullness thereof, the world and those who dwell therein" (Ps 24:1).

As the independent creator of all things, God also owns all things. He even owns the place where you live. All of your use, enjoyment, and abuse are accountable to him and the pleasure and purpose for which he created it. And when it flourishes, as God intended, we find more enjoyment and more health.

The children in year two of Creation Care Camp learned these lessons well. Year two helps them to see how all the animals, bugs, and plants have been designed by God to benefit each other. God put the kids, the animals, the bugs, and the plants in this particular place at this particular time. All of it belongs to him, and it glorifies him when it is thriving. Of course, it is simplest for the kids to see while eating, so each day's snack goes along with the theme of the day. When observing wheat grow, we eat bread, that kind of thing. I find it to be quite genius myself, and quite tasty. The last day of camp, I made bread, and Leslie brought cream from her cow, Sonny, a

---

4. Schaeffer, *Pollution and the Death of Man*, 54.

I Walk in My Garden in the Cool of the Day

dark-haired miniature Hereford standing about chest high on your average adult. Sonny often provides cream for coffee on Sunday morning. The kids learned about milking, and how to help Sonny stay healthy so she can, as the cattle manager taught us, turn grass that we can't eat into milk that we can. They took that milk and churned butter, which went onto the bread and into their mouths. Talk about happy kids! And what did they learn from the simple practice of being outside and getting their hands on it? Now, first let me insist that the time and the effort to care for Sonny and to produce milk and butter was beautiful in its own right, even if no "lesson" came out of it. But this was at camp, and there was a lesson. They learned that God created Sonny and owns her, that Leslie has a responsibility to God for the way Sonny lives and thrives. They learned that God is glorified when Sonny is flourishing as God intended, and they learned that when cows flourish, we are happy, too. Starting with what God wanted for Sonny actually made them happier.

We make a common human mistake when we start with ourselves and hear the charge to exercise dominion in God's world as if it were free reign to do as we like with it, but it is not possible to get that from the Bible as we have it. There is honestly no hint of that from Genesis 1 or 2, but there is from Genesis 3, in the mouth of the serpent calling Eve to throw off the rule of God and become an independent arbiter of good and evil. In the "good" creation of Genesis 1 and 2, our dominion is in light of God's dominion. God never walks away and asks Adam and Eve to handle it. The image of God in Adam and Eve, and in us, is representative. Your dominion is only and always under the dominion of God. That is, you have the power and right to do what God would do if he were in your place with your people.

In Genesis 3, it is the devil himself who suggests that our human rule is independent of God, as if we could ever have sufficient wisdom to bring about blessing and goodness on our own. It is just as much the devil's lie to say that mankind has free dominion as it is to say that the world exists without God. The dominion given to mankind is always and only under God's dominion.

God owns the garden you walk out into in the cool of the day. Whether you designed it yourself or inherited it with the house like I did, you still inherited it. The garden paths are there to lead you to flourish among your people and your place. You will show as much respect for your place as you have for the one who owns it. God created it and maintains all rights over

God sends people to restore places

it. He desires that all who worship him take pleasure in his world and join in the purpose he has for it.

Chapter 5

Going to Seed

Our children have always taken part in the hard work of gardening. From planting the seeds to tilling the plot, they get their hands dirty and enjoy the produce. We have learned together to break out of the supermarket aisle produce box. We were born and bred suburbanites longing for a country way of life. That made us the butt of many country jokes when we first arrived. I cannot tell you how many times I've been called a "city boy." But how were we supposed to know? Why did no one ever tell us that artichokes grow upside down with their points up? Or that carrots came in white and yellow? Or that there are over 5,000 varieties of tomatoes? The garden is an amazing world of abundance. We tend to plant everything by color in the garden we inherited, just for the sheer pleasure of it. Last spring, we planted red popcorn, orange tomatoes, purple potatoes, and purple bush beans—which are different from pole beans, if you didn't know—black garbanzo beans, yellow cucumbers, and white melons. Not to mention the annual grapes in three colors, berries in two, and onions in four. We praise God for a garden full of color that Crayola could never even come close to.

In the garden, the beets are already praising God. It is we who have to catch up. They praise him as they form that magnificent ball-shaped root the color that would honor any king's robe. That color stains our children's hands with the pleasures of God as we cut them open and taste the small shavings without even bothering to brush away all the soil. And they praise him by growing leafy greens that your mother always insisted were good for fiber, as if somehow the knowledge of an improved digestive system would make them seem more appealing. No, it is not the "nutritional benefit" that causes us to join in the praise; it's the taste! Roast those roots into caramelized wonderfulness and toss those greens with a little olive oil, and you cannot help but raise your hands to heaven in gratitude to God for a world that tastes good!

We let the beets go to seed the first year, just from not knowing when to harvest them. Long spindly stems shot up, twisting and turning around each other like red and green flames in the garden, flickering their delight toward heaven. Each stem, covered in seed, dropped its payload into the bed below. After the first good rain, beets started growing everywhere! We were both shocked and delighted. I reluctantly thinned the free shoots of glory into neat rows, a reasonable distance apart, and then we entered once again into the liturgy of the garden, praising the Lord up with the greens and down with the roots. In the first garden, *good* brought pleasure to God and man; in this garden, it brings pleasure to this man and his family.

God takes pleasure in your place

In the first garden, everything that the Lord God made was good, good and very good. Light? That's good. Water and dry land? They are good. Sun, moon, and stars? You get the picture. But what does it mean for the creeping things to be good in that magnificent place where nothing is yet bad? What does it even mean to be "good" when there is no "bad" to set in contrast? It means that they reflect God accurately; they tell us something true about God or as King David writes later, "There is no speech, their voice is not heard," yet "Their line has gone out through all the earth, And their utterances to the end of the world" (Ps 19:3–4). The lilies of the field are beautiful, blessed, and fruitful when they simply praise him by showing his glory to all who would pass by.

Going to Seed

The unnamed psalmist joins in the praise of creation in Psalm 148:

> Praise the Lord!
> Praise the Lord from the heavens;
> praise him in the heights!
> Praise him, all his angels;
> praise him, all his hosts!
> Praise him, sun and moon,
> praise him, all you shining stars!
> Praise him, you highest heavens,
> and you waters above the heavens!
> Let them praise the name of the Lord!
> For he commanded and they were created.
> And he established them forever and ever;
> he gave a decree, and it shall not pass away.
> Praise the Lord from the earth,
> you great sea creatures and all deeps,
> fire and hail, snow and mist,
> stormy wind fulfilling his word!
> Mountains and all hills,
> fruit trees and all cedars!
> Beasts and all livestock,
> creeping things and flying birds!
> Kings of the earth and all peoples,
> princes and all rulers of the earth!
> Young men and maidens together,
> old men and children!
> Let them praise the name of the Lord,
> for his name alone is exalted;
> his majesty is above earth and heaven.
> He has raised up a horn for his people,
> praise for all his saints,
> for the people of Israel who are near to him.
> Praise the Lord!

Notice that there is really only one purpose here, and it is praise. Every creature praises their creator, from the soil to the plants, from bugs to the animals, from the kings to the young men with their maidens. They praise in their purpose and their praise brings God pleasure. That original garden was a place of immense pleasure for God and for *everything* and *everyone* as each one simply lived out their part in the garden of God. Just think about that; God did not have to make our world pleasing. He did it because he wanted to.

God sends people to restore places

Pastor and author John Piper dedicates an entire chapter of his book, *The Pleasures of God,* to the theme of God's pleasure in God's own creation. This book sparked that "I wonder how dirt and God will come together in my life" when I first read it. Seeing the magnificence and joy that God knows in himself made me grateful to be a believer. It lifted my young Christian eyes up beyond thankfulness for freedom from sin and a life of bondage to the greatest gift, that is, God himself. I get God . . . and I am filled with joy. One passage, in particular, put my feet on the ground with that joy. It taught me to follow Jesus all the way down to the dirt. He tells of the day that the *Ranger Rick* journal arrived at the house for his kids. *Ranger Rick*, he says, is a theological journal.

> Ranger Rick arrives in our house. I open it and read about the European water spider that lives at the bottom of a lake, but breathes air. It does a somersault on the surface of the water and catches a bubble of air, and holds it over the breathing holes in the middle of its body while it swims to the bottom of the lake and spins a silk web among the seaweed. Then it goes up and brings down bubble after bubble until a little balloon of air is formed where it can live and eat and mate.
>
> I sit there with my mouth open and I think God smiles and says, "Yes, John, and I have been enjoying that little piece of art for 10,000 years before anybody on earth knew it existed. And if you only knew how many millions of other wonders there are beyond your sight that I behold with gladness everyday!"[1]

I get it. I always have to some degree. Starting with Mt. Baldy, the Devil's Bathtub, and my own garden. The pleasures of God are found in his handiwork.

Many years after reading about the pleasure to be found in *Ranger Rick*, I sat in the waiting room of a doctors office while a team of medical professionals performed tests on my wife to determine whether she had cancer. They said there was not enough space in the room for me to come along, and there was too much concern for infection for me to be close enough to hold her hand. So, she went in alone, and I sat in the waiting room with her mother, both of us feeling more alone than we knew what to do with. On the table next to me was an old copy of *Ranger Rick*, from December 1994, old enough to be the copy Pastor John was talking about. There was a white bird on the cover and joy between the pages. While I still

---

1. Piper, *The Pleasures of God*, 90.

did not know what was going on in the doctor's office, I felt the pleasure of God, proven by his creation. We are grateful to God that, after many tests, the doctors found no cancer and I continue to be grateful for the comfort provided by creation that day.

This is how I feel in my garden everyday. I know that, factually, God is not nearer to me there than in my study or in the post office, but I am more alert to his pleasures there. Each piece of broken eggshell in the compost causes me to leap inside and each worm draws a response like it did for Carter and Sophia at Creation Care Camp when they unearthed a worm in the raised bed garden. You would have thought they discovered the earth's greatest treasure. In a way, they did.

God has plans for your place

Mankind was placed into this garden and told to cultivate it, to serve it, to ensure that God's glory showed forth. This was to be their act of dominion . . . this was their original purpose. God planned for his creation to flourish natively in human hands. And to ensure they did not confuse the call to act on God's behalf towards his creation with the free reign in the candy shop, God gave a command. One simple command, just enough to say, "It still belongs to me. You still belong to me. Your dominion is under my dominion." That command was, in essence, "Don't eat from that tree; it will kill you."

It is in this garden that the devil serpent enticed Eve and Adam to an autonomous life, exercising their own dominion in their place. Sure, they became independent, but they lost their flourishing relationship with their good God, their good place, and with each other. Guilt entered their world, along with shame and blame. They lost the pleasure as well as their purpose. In God's world, our dominion is always under dominion. We always work for him and towards his ends. It is the devil's lie that tells us otherwise. Straight from his evil tongue, full of deadly poison, set ablaze by the fires of Hell itself.

God created the world to display his eternal goodness for all to see. He saw it, and he saw that it was good. He created you, those oak trees on my hillside, and me, so that whoever has eyes to see would find his glory reflected in them. When we see that reflection accurately, we will praise him with great joy and gratitude just because it wells up within us like a fountain about to overflow. While it may have seemed like he moved on to plan B after Adam and Eve's rebellion brought about death and destruction, he did not. God will bring more good and display more beauty through redeeming lost sinners and a broken creation than you and I could have ever imagined possible, but more on that to follow.

My daughter Meg forages the back alleys of town with joy, almost as if all the fruit trees in the world were purposefully planted just for her. She has learned from her fantastic and resourceful riding instructor that our small town is a moving feast, always in season, when you travel by horseback. I walk with her; I don't ride. I mean—I do not ride. I've been terrified of horses since I was thirteen. I am convinced that those enormous creatures are plotting a way to eat me. But the kids are horsemen, and they are good. I love watching the joy on their faces when they ride, and even when they clean the pens. If only I could find a way to make chores at home that much fun. There are days when they come home from a ride, filthy and bruised. "How was the ride?" I ask. "Good," Meg might answer nonchalantly, "we rode through the creek bareback and then practiced mounted archery in the arena." As if these things are just what normal people do every day. They have gone to seed in Santa Margarita, feeling God's pleasure in the purpose of his place.

One day, I was in my study preparing the Sunday sermon, only to look up in response to a neighing sound at the screen. There, almost inside my study, were two massive horse heads, with Meg and Leia, her instructor, bending down to look in. The ladies were laughing hysterically as I nearly fell off my chair. Leia thinks it's funny to get the horses as close to me as possible to see which one of us will empty our bladder first . . . the horse usually wins.

So, I was walking with Meg through the alleys and pathways of our small western town, and she fed me all the way along. She picked chamomile growing along the path; it was a pungent kind of taste, like you would assume if you've enjoyed it as a tea. In the alley between H and J Streets, we ate from an apricot tree, one of the earlier of the fruit trees to bloom. She pointed out that there are peaches, plums, berries, figs, apples, pears, kumquats, pomegranates, and persimmons—all that hang over backyard fences like the levitical corners of the field left behind to feed hungry neighbors, just as God intended.

God's intention is still for the created world to act as a theater of his divine goodness and pleasure, especially the part of it you live in. Do you see where we are going with this? Here is how the logic goes:

Going to Seed

1. *Since* our God created all things, *then* he also owns all things.
2. *Since* he owns your place in particular, *then* you must bow before his ownership and seek to work in your part of the world toward his ends.
3. *Since* his ends are his pleasure, *then* they will be your pleasure, too.

However, some things need to be repurposed in a fallen world. Some things no longer flourish natively, and so we enter in and repurpose them. Repurposing is good. God likes repurposing. The last weekend of September is Savor Weekend in Santa Margarita. Savor the Central Coast is a food and wine event sponsored by *Sunset Magazine* at venues throughout the county. The main event takes place on our ranch; backyard garden demonstrations, professional chefs, food and wine tasting, all representing our local area. You walk in with your boots on, if you know what you're doing; it is a ranch, after all, even though it is dressed up for a party. Entering through the great, bannered pavilion the old steam engine roars by like you just stepped back in time. To your left lie the Estrada Gardens, named after the original owner of the Rancho, now designed for weddings. The Gardens, filled with people and live music, provide tastes of good local food and locally brewed beer. Just to the right, under the hay shelter roof, runs restaurant stand after stand hawking single bites of pure joy, encapsulating the skill of each chef in a mouthful.

As a thank you to our small town for allowing 8,000 visitors for the weekend, the sponsors of the event give our town a booth space in their exhibition tent. Picture a circus tent filled with small representations of Central Coast communities seeking tourism and a crowd that has had one, two, or three too many glasses of wine. When *Sunset* first made the booth space offer, a few of us gathered together over a cup of coffee at The Porch and asked, "How do we best represent our town?" And how do we do it on purpose? After some brainstorming and some sketching, we headed out to the Santa Margarita Ranch woodpile where they said we could help ourselves to what we needed. Now, by woodpile, I do not mean a stack of cordwood to heat the house in the winter. I mean a half-acre spread of wooden leftovers that have gathered there over the centuries: 2 x 4's; old flooring from what could have been the house of the blacksmith on I Street; doors with leaded glass, maybe from one of the old Margarita hotels; and arched window frames from a church that stood somewhere near here in years gone by. My mind started constructing a new community church from those arches. Taking advantage of Tom Smith's playful imagination, we repurposed what we needed to construct a movable replica of an old western shop like what used to be on the El Camino Real, which passes through our town. One weekend a year, volunteers man that booth to brag about our little town to anyone who will stop and listen. "Do you want to know a little more about the town you're in?" we ask, as folks walk by. And the interested get more than they bargained for about The Range restaurant, Margarita Adventures, and the history of a place that still lives its history.

I am convinced that there is no one better at this job than me. This is not all at true. Cheri is amazing at telling the town history, and Nick and Mary make everyone feel that they belong the moment they enter the booth. But I have become Santa Margarita's biggest fan. I've gone to seed, roots going down and shoots going up. I belong here. I think that is what God intends for each of us in our place, that we would so enjoy the people and the place where he has us that we would overflow with his praise until everyone and everything is flourishing.

God owns the place where you live and intends it to reflect his divine goodness to the people who live there with you. They should see his goodness in both what he created to be there and in the way that you live there. God intends that all people in all places would worship him. This is the church's missionary commission for every people in every place.

The sum of all things

God created the place where you live. He owns it, has plans for it, *and* he takes pleasures in it. God sent you to that place to work it, to cultivate it, so that his goodness will be better reflected when you leave than it was when you arrived. It is not just your home; it is God's home. You are called to act as God would have you act towards it. You are his representative, his steward in every aspect of your life there.

God owns the food you eat, the fuel you use to drive, and the water you use to bathe. You are not permitted to take your identity from it as an "environmentalist." This is the concern that causes some Christians to push back when we talk about creation care. There has been a real pagan influence in the environmental movement. That is a very valid concern. However, you do not need to worry about being defiled. Jesus' sacrifice for you cannot be diminished by friendship with those who worship wrongly and act in unbelief. Trust what Jesus has accomplished for you already. You must remember that there is nothing in this world that can separate you

Going to Seed

from the love of Christ. God is pleased with you because of the substitutionary sacrifice of Jesus, not because of your abstinence from pagan influence. Jesus came into the world to save sinners, not pretty good cultural Christians.

On the other hand, without this belief in God as owner, it is possible to feel free to use the world for your own ends. You could see everything simply as a "natural resource" to be exploited because it's all going to burn one day anyway. But it is not a resource; it's a tree, and God owns it. It's not "biomass." It's the flesh of a cow, and God owns it. The man or woman who eats God's creatures is obligated to use that nourishment for God's purposes. God owns the world and fully expects his people to use it towards his ends. To do anything else would be sin. Not just damaging, but sin. That is why worship is the primary call of the local church in regards to creation care. Start here: repent of believing that Jesus' death was less powerful than a political movement; believe a strong and sufficient gospel, yes your sins have been strong, but your Christ is stronger; now live consistently with that gospel in all of life, in relation to your people and your place.

With that confidence, go and address the false religion that accompanies much of the environmental movement by living consistently with your own faith and by challenging the inconsistency of theirs. True ecological/environmental change will only occur when we stop worshipping self or the environment and begin worshipping the God who created all things, owns all things, and has an end for which he created all things.

Some of you might be asking, "Aren't Christians coming in late to this environmental game?" Organizationally, as American evangelicals, perhaps In all other senses, no. The natural connection between the created world and faith was not only seen in the teaching of Jesus but immediately understood by the early church. Just one example, Basil the Great, an early church leader from the fourth century, wrote,

> I want creation to penetrate you with so much admiration that wherever you go, the least plant may bring you the clear remembrance of the Creator.... One blade of grass or one speck of dust is enough to occupy your entire mind in beholding the art with which it has been made.[2]

Christians have always understood that the God who created the heavens and the earth also cares for what he made. Though, as we are seeing, the

---

2. Quoted in Faw, "A Brief Theology of Creation Care."

idea of "caring" means something different than if you start without God, that is, if you start with yourself as the center of all things. To care is to help restore people and places to God's intended wholeness. God has a purpose; to care for creation is to join that purpose for both our people and our place.

One modern organizational example of Christians caring for people and their places is A Rocha, to which I belong. A Rocha is an international Christian nature conservation organization with projects in twenty countries on five continents. A Rocha (uh RAW-sha), Portuguese for "The Rock," founded by Anglican missionaries to Portugal, has been caring for people and place for over thirty years. A Rocha seeks God's purpose in all of those places by conducting scientific research, running hands-on conservation projects, and operating environmental education programs to improve the well-being of both the people and the place. As one of the world's largest and oldest Christian conservation organizations, and as the only Christian organizational member of the International Union for the Conservation of Nature, A Rocha is uniquely qualified to partner with the local church to put people and place back together. We have years of experience in restoring hearts through faith in the gospel that then restore the place where God has sent them, achieving God's purpose at the same time. That is to say, if you need help, ask. We've been doing this, all over the world, for a long time.

But, aren't we supposed to be focusing on people? Isn't this a distraction from the church's evangelistic task? Perhaps, anything can be. But first, be sure you are not using this as a scapegoat. Are you really running out of time to evangelize? Are you evangelizing so often that you don't have time to care for your place? Really? That is not actually an issue, is it? The truth is that we have enough time and resources to bring the good news to our neighbors and live in our place in such a way that it brings good to all creation. A demonstrable love for people and place will only serve your evangelism. A pastor friend of mine likes to say, "We do good works, which create good will upon which we share the good news." I am convinced that Peter and Miranda Harris have had the opportunity to share the gospel of salvation with more people because they have banded—caught, tagged and released—100,000 birds than they would have if they stayed behind a church pulpit.

When we believe that God owns the place, we find our pleasure tied to his purposes in creation, and worship will always be our first response, just as it is for the trees and the mountains. Then, and only then, will people and place be put back together. Do you believe this? Will you live in your place for God's purpose and God's pleasures? Will you follow him all the way down to the dirt?

God restores people

The difference between what God created us to be and do and what we actually are and do is what is wrong with our world. That is, the problem is localized within our hearts even before it is systemic and worldwide. God's first work of both social and ecological restoration is restoring our hearts through redeeming grace that comes by faith in Jesus Christ as Savior.

God's new people

Chapter 6

Manure is Compost, Not Fertilizer

I have killed two and two-thirds apples trees since I've lived in Santa Margarita. I planted two of them myself, one back towards the chicken coop and the other over on the far side of the circle pathway, trying to keep the old one company. The two, a Braeburn and Granny Smith, were chosen for a children's illustration at our annual church in the park service. Each year, at the end of summer we gather for Sunday worship in the Santa Margarita Community Park to celebrate. We Campbells rejoice on that day because it is the anniversary of our first Sunday in Santa Margarita. But the church gathers to celebrate what God has done in us, the church, and especially in our church children over the last year. Fall begins the new Sunday school year, and kids move up from Bible stories to learning the catechism or from learning the catechism to learning to question the catechism in a healthy way. They are going to ask questions, so we teach them to ask good ones. Anyone can ask "What does that mean?" But we want our kids to also ask, "And how does that work with this other truth I have been learning?" Good question-askers have healthier roots.

God restores people

On the year of the apple trees, we were remembering our summer lessons by speaking about the two trees at the ends of the Bible, one tree of life in the garden of Eden and another in the garden city. The kids climbed up the stairs of the old gazebo one at a time and told the stories of what they had learned. It's a wonderful gazebo, like you might imagine in a rural country park, just maybe a little more worn and weathered. The brown paint on the lower half is more peeled than present. The white paint on top is only called white because we know it was white at one time. The rail on the right side gives way a bit when you lean against it. When you're not leaning against it, it looks great. Metal flashing forms the edges of the stairs, helping them to stay together under the onslaught of little feet day after day, and on this day, many little feet pounded their way to the top and to the microphone.

"Before the beginning, God existed," recited one.

"In the beginning, God created the heavens and the earth," proclaimed another, with the confidence of Martin Luther's "Here I stand." With this, the Granny Smith was displayed as a symbol of the universe that God created, though he himself already existed prior to the Granny Smith. One has to wonder if a Granny Smith would have been enough of a temptation to lead to the fall of humanity.

"One day, God will make all things right," chanted several together to end the recitation around the Braeburn, which the tree in the heavenly garden is sure to be, yielding its fruit in season.

And the congregation, seated under the shade of the fruitless mulberries, stood from their folding chairs and cheered the fruit in the lives of our children.

Simone at the Educated Gardener, which we all call EdGar, helped pick out the two trees. This fantasyland of a nursery boasts several whimsically designed water ponds, as well as lovely little places to sit, either in the warm sun or under a bowing tree. You wander that happy space among outbuildings that would make any Disney Imagineer jealous. They serve as Simone's office, storage, an aviary, a place for conducting business, and another for taking care of your business if you must. Passing through the gates and by the towering sunflower sculpture, built from old bicycle wheel rims, you are greeted by Jinx the cat, Chicken John, and, of course, Simone. Simone *is* gardening in Santa Margarita. She knows our soils and our microclimates. And if she does not know, she will find out. For example, I asked for her help to plant a gooseberry patch in our garden, along the back

Manure is Compost, Not Fertilizer

of the house, beneath the bedroom windows. My wife's Danish family loves gooseberries and this patch was to be in honor of her father. Simone did the research to find out that the Pixwell variety would do just fine in our zone and had them delivered to her shop for me to pick up. We often speak about how those berries are doing; they should bear fruit this coming spring for the first time.

Simone helped me pick out those two apple trees with the intent that I would plant them in the backyard after the illustration. I did. The Granny Smith died that fall. I couldn't even keep it alive as long as Adam and Eve could keep away from the Tree of the Knowledge of Good and Evil. I'm honestly still not sure what went wrong, but it is dead and that way to the garden is blocked forever. The Braeburn bore fruit this year, but before harvest time, it caught a disease that started over on the grape vines. I am hoping it isn't actually dead. Braeburn apples are a foretaste of heaven you know.

The last apple tree I killed was the one Sharon left in the garden. It was a beautiful little tree, grafted with three types of fruit. A triangular pattern of branches separate out from the stock like they are taking the first step on a thousand-mile journey to different places, hither and yon, into the exotic lands of appledom. The document Sharon left, naming all things in her garden, simply calls it the "3-in-1 Apple Tree." Today, a yellow fungus grows on the fruitless branches; some wood has clearly died and bark keeps peeling away like leprosy. The tree never produces any actual fruit; some started once, but none have made it to harvest. Two areas low down on the tree continue to leaf out every year. They set groupings of five or six apples in a bunch, but never finish. Two of the three grafts were really gone since before I arrived. I've been nurturing the third; pruning, treating, and feeding with both store-bought products and the produce of local horses. Manure, I am told, is compost, not fertilizer. It is much too hot, with too much nitrogen, but when you start with the long slow mellowing of the compost pile, a fruitful life can come of it.

Jesus told a parable in the Gospel of Luke about a fruitless fig tree as a way of calling his followers to repentance.

> And He began telling this parable: "A man had a fig tree which had been planted in his vineyard; and he came looking for fruit on it and did not find any. And he said to the vineyard-keeper, 'Behold, for three years I have come looking for fruit on this fig tree without finding any. Cut it down! Why does it even use up the ground?'

69

God restores people

> "And he answered and said to him, 'Let it alone, sir, for this year too, until I dig around it and put in fertilizer; and if it bears fruit next year, fine; but if not, cut it down'" (Luke 13:6–9).

Jesus' aim is for the fig tree, a common metaphor for Old Testament Israel, to bear fruit, not for it to be chopped down. The parable extends that same hope to you and me, that we would be fruitful. The fruit of churches restoring people and places starts with churches of restored people. That is, the way of restoration starts with you being restored to relationship with God and the world, either for the first time or in a deeper and more mature way. The fruit of restoration starts with shoveling loads of composted manure around your roots.

Taking Root

Apples grow well in our microclimate, but citrus does not. Everyone tries to keep a lemon tree, usually a dwarf, in a pot on wheels so that it can be moved under cover when the frost comes. In our neck of the woods, first frost averages November 7, and last frost April 15. What grows really well here are the California Walnut, *Juglans Californica*. Actually, they grow like weeds. One is currently tearing out the fence between my house and my neighbor's thanks to some passing bird that dropped a nut at the wrong time in flight. Crows gather the walnuts and drop them in the street just before cars pass by, turning the cars into mobile nutcrackers in the service of the feathery beasts. Crows and squirrels love the nuts, but they are not very good for human consumption. Folks here will graft a branch from a walnut tree that is native to England onto the trunk of a native California walnut and that combination thrives together. One tastes great, and the other grows great in this soil and climate. Starting with the right root stock in the right climate leads to good fruit.

You live some place. It is a real place, even if it feels like everyplace else. It has a climate. It has a soil content, and there are trees that will grow there, ones that will not grow here for me. Your place is a unique place, even if you live in the kind of town where your suburban strip mall with a restaurant, clothing chain, and some version of a drug store, could be uprooted out of any other suburban context, anywhere else in the world. It is a real and lively community. James Howard Kuntsler, in his typical wit that crosses the line at times, speaks of community in a very physical, placed kind of way.

Manure is Compost, Not Fertilizer

> Community is not something you have, like pizza. Nor is it something you can buy. It's a living organism based on a web of interdependencies—which is to say, a local economy. It expresses itself physically as connectedness, as buildings actively relating to each other, and to whatever public space exists, be it the street, or the courthouse or the village green.[1]

Your community has a name. It has borders; it has water, trees, and people. God walks there in your lives, his local church, filled with his Spirit. Most importantly, your place has *you* because God put you there. God owns your place and he put you there with purpose. As John Stott puts it, "The Earth belongs to God by creation and to us by delegation."[2]

Whether you believe that or not will shape both what kind of trees you plant and the way you live in your place. The old saying, "What we believe comes out our fingertips" is never more true than ecologically. If you believe that God owns all things and that he has sent you to care for both your people and your place, then you will live like God owns the place. Any ecological good that you can do must come from this kind of thinking and from a heart that worships the one true God. Christian ecology starts as an act of worship that becomes an act of discipleship. Discipleship in the local church restores and reroots people; then restored and rooted people restore places.

Rooting God's people

Where do we find ourselves in this purpose of God in God's world? How do we begin to live our actual daily lives in our actual daily place as restored disciples of Jesus, all the way down to the dirt?

We begin with the heart of the matter; we begin with God because God begins with God. In our brokenness, we all tend to think that it all starts with us. Whether you are a rich young ruler or a poor and persevering widow, it is part of our fallen spiritual DNA to act as if the world revolves around us. As if it rose when we were born and will set when we die. All that is, people and place, exist to serve our ends and us. That is impossible, of course, and quite silly when you say it out loud. As novelist Sylvia Plath

---

1. Kunstler, *The Geography of Nowhere*, 185.
2. Stott, *The Radical Disciple*, 51.

God restores people

has said on behalf of all humans, "I took a deep breath and listened to the old brag of my heart; I am, I am, I am."[3]

Fortunately for the world, this is not true. As God's people we know that all things start with God. We know that there was a beginning to all things, and before that beginning, there was nothing. I mean if you draw a circle and inside the circle write "everything," you would have to erase the "everything" and then erase the circle. There was a time when there was not time, there was not space, there was not stuff, there was nothing. And God was already there. To build a life, a marriage, a community, or an environment, the one true God must be the first building block. This we know by revelation, and starting here is the right root to bear good fruit. It takes faith to start with God, but it takes even more to start with yourself.

We know, practically, that our story does not start with us. We have arrived at the end of a very long line of history, people, and events in this place, the place where God brought us with purpose. The Apostle Paul offers a prime example of the truth that it did not start with us in the book of Acts chapter 17. Remember the context of Paul's sermon on Mars Hill. He has been on one of his missionary journeys, traveling from country to country declaring the good news that God became man in Jesus, walked the dirt among us, living a righteous life and dying a sacrificial death. Jesus lived the life we should have lived and died the death we should have died. Even better, God raised Jesus from the dead again, proving that he was truly God become man and that he did truly save us from our sins. The God who made all things was made man, then was unmade so that we and all things might be remade.

Having escaped a threat on his life in the city of Berea, Paul finds himself alone in Athens where he wanders around, seeing the sights. He observed that the city was "full of idols" so he engaged a group of gathered free thinkers in a wholehearted discussion of the gospel. His message started with God, the "God who made the world and all that is in it" (17:24). This is the God who is "Lord of heaven and earth," so he does not need anything, "nor is He served by our hands as if he needed anything" (17:25). In reality, it is he who gives "life and breath and all things" (17:26). It is he who,

> made from one man every nation of mankind to live on all the face of the earth, having determined their appointed times and the boundaries of their habitation (17:26).

3. Plath, *The Bell Jar*, 256.

Do you see it? God has determined for you to be in your place at this time, even though much history has passed before you arrived here. Empires have conquered, been conquered, and then faded away. Philosophers have discovered the answer to all things metaphysical, and then another philosopher discovered that they were wrong. Lovers have wooed, loved, bore children, and left the world with just a bit more color than when they arrived. Julius Caesar has gone before us. Descartes has been here and so has John Donne. All of those things precede us. They are gifts to us and we had nothing to do with making them happen. We just receive them, and we receive the responsibility to steward them, to bear fruit in the garden with both the good soil and the manure that we've been planted in.

There has been much life in this place, both ecologically and spiritually that has taken place before I arrived. I know this, but my own sinfulness lures me into believing that "I think therefore I am" is a sufficient starting point. The climate of our place started long before we arrived, long before Caesar's Rome, Descartes's humanism, or Donne's poetry. We are joining a program already in progress. This is the most fundamental truth of our Christian conversion and absolutely essential for living consistently. When we start our thinking, especially ecological thinking, with ourselves instead of starting with God, we will fail to bear the fruit of image-bearing people in our place. We are his image bearers, his divine representatives, to act as God would act if he lived in this place, though we do not represent him as we ought and we do not relate as he created us to related.

Restored to represent God

Starting with the fact God's existence and the story of him remaking the world will actually restore us where we are broken, where the bark on our limbs is leprous and peeling and the fruit sets but never makes harvest. That is where we need to be restored, made again, like we were created to be in the first garden.

You and I were created by God to live abundantly in our places, bearing the fruit of the divine life he has given us. We were created to enjoy the very good creation of God, cultivating and keeping it, resting and worshipping God on the seventh day in the garden of Eden. We were created to send down roots and send out fruits. *But* instead of living abundant lives of faith that flow out of roots set deep in God, we daily choose to die the death of sinful Adam by believing the promises of sin more than the promises of God. We choose to plant a California Redwood in a neighborhood in which it wasn't made to thrive. That Redwood will grow, and it will grow to enormous heights, but it will take an equally enormous amount of water. The tree is not native. When we start with ourselves, as we have since the fall, we cannot act as God would act, and we cannot restore people and places.

We were created to think God's true thoughts after him. We were created to know him and his ways by conscience, creation, and by holy revelation. Knowing we are creatures and not the creator, we should refuse to even pretend that we are adequate to judge what is good and what is evil. If we were still healthy trees, we would plant ourselves by streams of water. We would meditate on his Word day and night. *But* instead of thinking God's thoughts after him, we suppress God's truth because we prefer unrighteousness. Instead of doing what are told, we plant an orchard of pomegranates on the corner lot in the center of town. Let me tell you a story about my good friend that I think is a good example of how we respond to the commands of God. He wanted to develop his lot in town, but the regulations between the county and the state governments became too demanding. So, he planted a pomegranate orchard instead. He built a beautiful fence around the property and then added a windmill and water tower to make it a scenic spot in the middle of town. Last year, I married him and his lovely wife in front of that water tower, beside the blossoming fruit trees. Then, on the pronouncement of man and wife, the bagpipes started up and marched the whole congregation down the street to the pub. Yes, that really happened, right here in Santa Margarita. That is how we begin what hopes to be a healthy and fruitful marriage where I come from. That does not need regulation.

We were created to worship God, as we are the only spiritual beings in all of creation. We were created to respond to him and his good gifts with gratitude and overflowing praise. We were created to be well watered like a fast growing Cottonwood that claps its hands as a standing ovation in the fall wind, just before dropping its leaves at the final curtain of the season. *But* we have become idolaters and we worship the creatures rather than the creator who is forever praised, amen. Instead of lifting our hands in praise because of the beautiful blossoms, we tear the tree down because of the mess of falling fruit, like that tree someone stole from the front of the church. Two magnificent trees once stood out front of the cute little nightmare, guarding the walkway like ancient soldiers. In the spring, the sentry on the left would deck itself out in white and the soldier on the right in bright pink. We arrived for church one Sunday and the faithful white protector had vanished and no one knew what happened. We wondered with a mixture of panic and frustration, who comes in the night and cuts down a tree? Here I was, a relatively new pastor in the church, just terrified that I would take the blame for the loss of the beloved old friend. Miss Hazel, the church matriarch, arrived to hear the morning commotion and declared with some force, "I had it cut down, the mess was too much when it was fruiting. And anyway, I carried the sprout up here in a shovel so I figured I could take it out." We will be replanting a Magnolia tree right there, in her honor.

We were created to act morally and rightly according to God's good character. We were created to do his will on earth as it is in heaven, to be the church bearing the good fruit of restoring people and place. *But* instead of acting rightly according to God's good ends for the people and place around us, we are immoral, and that adds daily to the brokenness around us. We grow where we want to grow without concern for the neighbors until the sidewalk beside the Pacific Beverage Distribution center buckles and bulges so much from Cottonwood roots searching for a water source, that it becomes a real hazard to the people of the place. When we start with ourselves, we do not represent God the way we were created to do. We do not bear the fruit we were created to bear.

Restored to relate

You can also see this same disease in our relationships. We were created to relate as God would have us relate, to God, ourselves, each other, and the rest of creation. You and I were created to take our personal identity from our relationship to God as his divine image bearers. We have a value beyond pure gold and cut diamonds because of that image; knowing this about ourselves frees us from the fear of loss because our own identity is firmly established in him and cannot be stolen by failures in either people or place. We have been given a value that is not added to by a good season of growth and not diminished during a barren season. But now, we are misdirecting our search for identity into affluence, work, broken relationships, and a false dominion over the world. We no longer know who we are as individual selves. We may be growing, but it is because our roots have tapped into the septic tank leach line. We may be producing fruit, but no one wants to eat it.

We were created to relate to one another like God the Son relates to God the Father. We were created to freely love others for their good without risk to ourselves because we are secure in the image of God and the redemption of Christ. Deep relational roots make the tree strong in the wind. *But* now, we demand others support *our* identity, bringing glory to us at great cost to themselves, like the poison oak that wraps itself around healthy live trees and slowly sucks the life out of them like a parasitic worm.

We were created to relate to our place as the representatives of God, bringing more good, more beauty, more fruitfulness to the place when we leave than when we arrived. But now, we are separated from God, ourselves, each other, and our world, yet we are still insisting on our own way. Instead of bringing in the compost, we just pile on the manure.

When the tree is not healthy, there will be no fruit. When the roots are bad, the tree will die. What I'm saying is that we need restoration ourselves if we are to be about the work of restoration.

Bloom where you are planted

This is the Bible's story of our earthly place. It belongs to God in whom we "live and move and have our being" (Acts 17:28). We are created to be his glorious, valuable, and perfectly equipped representatives. We are here to live fully, to relate deeply, and to function towards his ends for our place. It runs counter to the religion of other ecological stories that begin with either humanity as the problem or as the redeemer. *But it is true.* Whole life discipleship must start here, if we are to bear fruit. Our hearts need to be changed. If we are to restore, we need more compost and less manure.

Chapter 7

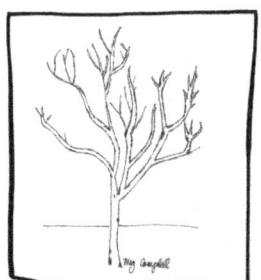

The Root of the Problem

The bus pulled into Santa Margarita like a three-ring circus. High school juniors unfolded like clowns emerging from their specialty car. They came from a Southern California city church to visit us out in the sticks. We were one of their summer mission projects and benefited from a traveling Vacation Bible School program complete with counselors, lesson plans, games, and props. All we had to do was add food and water. Splitting into teams, they fanned out through town knocking on doors and handing out flyers. They slept in the church, took over the community hall, and swarmed into the park on Margarita Monday, our biweekly summer community potluck. It was the talk of the town. This was such a wonderful gift to our small-town church and community. They loved us, served us, and introduced our children to Jesus. We loved them and gave them an authentic small-town welcome, so they came back again. Their first year in Margarita, you would have thought they stepped back in time, running down country roads and walking uninvited into Grandma Hazel's house to sing and play music with her. One of our young men was wearing a pair of sandals, which just happened to be in fashion. "You have Rainbow sandals here?" the concrete-raised youngster asked incredulously. To which the local man responded, "And we have running water, too." That is to say, dirt and horses, gardens and vineyards were entirely new to our visitors. Old people even seemed to be a novelty. They had certainly never pruned grapes before. So, when I took them out into my garden with my few happy vines and began to hack them back, they were a little fearful.

My two red flame vines with hardy twelve-year-old stocks grow up and then out before crisscrossing along guide wires to form a canopy. The twisting trained vines explode with leaf and fruit in early summer, clusters squeezed into each other and vines running down on to the ground where the chickens love to peck at the grape leaves. I picked up one of those long and healthy looking branches along the ground and whacked it off. Then another . . . and another.

"What if you cut too much?" they inquired with some urgency.

"But there are grapes on those long branches hanging down to the ground. Are you going to cut off the grapes, too?" Gasps emerged from their wide mouths and even wider eyes as small green clusters of fruit hit the ground.

Yes, the answer is that you do cut them back because the grapes that remain will get more energy from the plant and will produce better fruit on the day of harvest. All this was theory to them at this point as I hacked away in faith. From experience, I was trusting that the beautiful leaves and healthy fruit that was cut away would, in the long run, make the whole plant more fruitful.

Together, standing next to the massacred vines of green table grapes, turning slightly red in color, we read the description of the life of faith in John 15 as being like grape branches that bear fruit because they abide in the vine. Then the vinedresser then that fruitful branch and cuts away and prunes with some force and vigor. In the parable, we are the branches, and Jesus is the root of the vine in which we abide, continually fed by his divine life so that we bear fruit. God the Father deliberately prunes us so that we will be more fruitful. Sometimes he cuts off dead wood and we agree that this should happen. At other times, he cuts off green shoots and even small fruit that is starting to form. We don't like that. We don't like it because we don't believe him. We don't believe that all things start with God. We don't believe that people and place go together. We don't believe that God sent us there to restore. We don't believe that God owns the place. We don't believe that our hearts need to be restored. Put differently, we don't like it because we don't believe that he is a good gardener. We don't believe that the slow growth of compost is better in the long run than the quick spurt of Miracle-Gro, which Simone calls "plant cancer." God has an idea of what it looks like to be restored, to flourish, and it starts with some deep pruning with you and your heart.

Creation care as whole life discipleship through the local church is just like this. Something needs to change at the root if we, our people and our place, are going to be restored. For some of you that will mean uprooting the entire plant because the fruit is bad. For others, a hearty pruning may do the job just fine. But root change is what the church does best.

Bad fruits from bad roots

When grape vines don't flourish and bear fruit, there is a root problem. When the people around us and the places we live in do not flourish, there is another kind of root problem. That root problem is our sinful hearts. Bad fruit comes from a heart that starts with self—letting my first thought be about myself, my existence, my will—rather than with God. And that fruit always has devastating results on my people and my place.

We have already said that Adam, Eve, and all of us since have thrown off the dominion of God as the proper starting place of all things in the created universe. This bears fruit in the way I represent myself rather than God. That is, I do not function as I was created to function and do not work towards God's end of restoring all things to himself. This one difference, this root difference, determines the kind of fruit my life will bear. Specifically, starting with myself means that I selfishly think about my role in the neighborhood, instead of asking, "How can I help bring about good here?" I ask, "How can I keep bad from happening to myself and those I care about?" One is a positive, the other is a negative. One is good for Kirk and Ingrid, the other is just good for me.

Starting with myself means that I think selfishly about my environment—to use the word correctly, meaning the conditions in which I live—and instead of asking, "How do I help this creek to flourish as God created it to flourish?" I simply ask, "How do I keep it from flooding my backyard?" One results in a beautiful creek, teeming with flora and fauna, flowing smoothly through town. The other results in nothing at all until I am being threatened, and then it is probably too late. The brokenness of starting with myself has actual real consequences to those around me and eventually to myself, as well.

Broken relationships in my neighborhood are the bad fruit of my heart problems. Environmental damage in my neighborhood is the bad fruit of my heart problems. There needs to be a heart change. You and I need to change before these broken pieces can begin to be healed. What I am saying is that the problem with your place and mine is not a pragmatic problem first. It is a heart problem first, and a pragmatic problem second. Bad fruits reveals a hard heart and that requires require radical change, not just behavioral change. Author Paul David Tripp tells a fun story illustrating this truth.

> Let's say I have an apple tree in my backyard. Each year its apples are dry, wrinkled, brown and pulpy. After several seasons, my friend says, "It doesn't make any sense to have this huge tree and never be able to eat any apples. Can't you do something?" One day my friend looks out the window to see me in the yard, carrying branch cutters, an industrial grade staple gun, a ladder, and two bushels of apples.
>
> I climb the ladder, cut off all the pulpy apples, and staple shiny, red apples onto every branch of the tree. From a distance our tree looks like it is full of a beautiful harvest. But if you were my friend, what would you be thinking of me this moment?
>
> If a tree produces bad apples year after year, there is something drastically wrong with its system, down to its very roots. I won't solve the problem by stapling new apples onto the branches. They also will rot because they are not attached to a life-giving root system. And next spring, I will have the same problem again. I will not see a new crop of healthy apples because my solution has not gone to the heart of the problem. If the tree's roots remain unchanged, it will never produce good apples.
>
> The point is that, in personal ministry, much of what we do to produce growth and change in ourselves and others is little more than "fruit stapling." It attempts to exchange apples for apples without examining the heart, the root behind the behavior. This is the very thing for which Christ criticized the Pharisees. Change that ignores the heart will seldom transform the life. For a while, it may seem like the real thing, but it will prove temporary and cosmetic.[1]

---

1. Tripp, *Instruments in the Redeemer's Hands*, 63.

The Root of the Problem

There are real consequences in this world for your sin and mine. Nothing is disconnected. We may try to deny it by exporting our trash to another place or keeping our relationships virtual, but it's true nonetheless. If abiding in Christ, the vine, bears much fruit (John 15:4), then apart from being rooted in him we can do nothing. Those branches are cut off; then they dry up, and are cast into the fire to burn (John 15:5-6). Apart from him, we do very real harm to our people and our place. We must honestly admit that the environmental problems in our places are far deeper than the cosmetic troubles of bad habits and water pollution. They are deeply rooted in the hearts of the people and the place suffer along with us.

The ax is already at the root

Something needs to change, and it needs to change at the roots. The difference between the good fruit of restoration and the bad fruit of further alienation depends upon your roots. The difference between Yerba Buena Creek flooding or not is my heart. The difference between the red-legged frog thriving in our watershed is my heart. The difference between swimming in that creek or it being too poisoned from pesticide run-off is my heart. The difference between blue oaks making a comeback or disappearing altogether is my heart. What we plant and nurture is what we will harvest. If I plant a briar patch, I will never pick grapes. Jesus himself told this parable about the need for heart change, root change, to bring about fruit change.

> For there is no good tree which produces bad fruit, nor, on the other hand, a bad tree which produces good fruit. For each tree is known by its own fruit. For men do not gather figs from thorns, nor do they pick grapes from a briar bush. The good man out of the good treasure of his heart brings forth what is good; and the evil man out of the evil treasure brings forth what is evil; for his mouth speaks from that which fills his heart (Luke 6:43-45).

You need to become a different kind of tree. It's as simple as that. That is a work of God, the true vinedresser, who is gloried when we bear much fruit and so prove to be his disciples. Or, we do not bear this fruit and prove not to be his disciples. And in that case, Jesus warns,

God restores people

> Indeed the axe is already laid at the root of the trees; so every tree that does not bear good fruit is cut down and thrown into the fire (Luke 3:9).

I wrote an article I entitled "Why I Don't Care about Climate Change," with some tongue in cheek. Of course, I care about what is happening in our world and especially the effect that is having on those image bearers of God who are suffering because of it. What I don't care to do is to spend my life chasing symptoms rather than the cause. I don't care to chase the wrong problem. I care to address the root of the problem that will heal the fruit of the people and the place. So, rather than addressing symptoms, I am addressing you, the person whose actions are contributing to the effects of climate change and all manner of destructive impacts on our beautiful world. I care about your thinking that leads to those actions and, most importantly, I care about your heart that enables your thinking, that then justifies your actions and has global effects such as climate change, as well as small local effect, such as our Santa Margarita Lake watershed.

In northwest Washington, Dave Timmer leads a team from A Rocha USA to restore the Fishtrap Creek watershed. A watershed is the area of land from which water drains to a common point. The Fishtrap Creek watershed covers nearly thirty-seven square miles and is one of the largest lowland tributaries to the Nooksack River. A Rocha Canada works to restore and preserve the ecologically connected Little Campbell River watershed just north of the forty-ninth parallel.

The absence of sufficient canopy cover to shade the stream allows water temperatures to rise too high for juvenile salmon that natively spawn in the creek. Also, nitrate contamination from dairy livestock manure and fertilizer use causes some species of plants to overgrow and deplete the oxygen needed for aquatic organisms. Pesticide contamination from both agricultural and residential runoff (like when you fertilize your lawn) make their way into the creek and have lethal effects on the creatures that live there.

How are we to define the problem here on the Nooksack? Is the problem the use of pesticides? Is it invasive reed grasses accidentally brought in by travelers? Is it the many dairy farms of the region whose fecal coliform leech into the waters? If these are the problem, then the solution is to stop it or fix it. But who gets to judge? Who will be the determiner of ecological good versus evil? Who will take on the role of the serpent in the garden? The problem is bigger than our behavior. To focus solely on environmental

The Root of the Problem

behaviors can quickly lead to a cult-like legalism, setting up an imposed list of rules determined by all-knowing leaders who decide who can be "holy" and who can't. If you shop with a reusable bag, you're holy. If you use plastic, you go straight to ecological hell. But without addressing the sinful heart and the selfish mind, there is no redemption in the real world made up of sinners, not just wasters. We have to think more deeply than the overly simple, "green," quick and easy answers. No heart has ever been changed by reducing and reusing.

While there are many good and necessary actions to take, and we will address some of them later, that's too simple, isn't it? We all can see that with only basic common sense. If we fix one symptom, another will soon follow. The problem is much deeper than that, as bad as that is. The problem is not with the fruit, but with the roots. The Bible calls that problem sin. Sin is the root of the problem that leads to bad fruit in our earthly home. This thinking runs counter to the religion of other, more simplistic, ecological stories. *But it is true.* The root of the problem in Fishtrap Creek and the root of the problem where you live is you—your sinful heart, not just your cow manure.

What is the Bible's solution to sin? It is a Savior. The Apostle Paul reminds us that God sent his Son "when the fullness of the time came" (Gal 4:4) and "at just the right time" he died for the ungodly (Rom 5:6). He came to save us from the consequences of our sin and from our sinful selves. The Bible calls this *redemption* (Gal 4:5), the same word we use for recycling. God is taking something broken, your heart, and turning it into something whole again. God's solution to the ecology problem in your place is to restore you.

In fact, God's entire plan in sending you to that place in this time was that you would "seek him and perhaps find him" (Acts 17:27) so that you may be restored. Then restored people restore people and places. The only real ecological solution is when your heart is changed through faith in Jesus. Jesus is the one by whom, through whom, and for whom all things were created (Col 1:16). Jesus is the one incarnated into his creation to reconcile all things to himself (Col 1:20). Jesus is the new covenant-maker who removes your heart of stone and gives you a heart of flesh (Ezek 36:26). Jesus is the one who died so that broken people can be healed, so your brokenness can be healed. Filthy people can be washed; you can be washed. Guilty people can be forgiven; you can be forgiven. Hearts can be changed. Lives can be transformed. The real invasive thorns produced by the tree of

God restores people

your life can become real fruit, but only when your heart is changed. Do you believe this? Have you been redeemed?

Here is the first point: a bad tree needs to be redeemed. Your sinful heart needs to be made new by the Savior Jesus. Ask him to forgive your sin, especially the sin of starting with yourself, and to give you a new heart. Today, right now, while reading this, it is time to repent of your sin. That is, admit that your sinful beliefs about God and yourself and the actions that come from those beliefs are both wrong and destructive and agree to turn from them as God has commanded. Trust that God will forgive you because Jesus has taken the payment for your sin when he died on the cross, and he will restore your heart. Only a good heart will bear good fruit; only a restored person will restore places.

Prune our hearts, Lord

Sometimes, redeemed and restored people still fail to redeem and restore. You already believe that God is, that he has redeemed you, and that he is restoring all things. At least you give assent to those things, even if they do not bear fruit in your life. Like Judas from the Bible, you follow Jesus around, but he and his ways do not capture your heart. You see the beauty of both your people and your place, but cannot grasp that you might be damaging them and that God considers this to be sin. Your heart may require some pruning so that you may bear more fruit.

My daily commute takes five minutes, to walk from home to the church on the hill. We call it "the church on the hill" because it sits on the only hill in town, though it isn't much of a hill, honestly. The walk covers just two small town blocks and passes a handful of neighbors, all but one of whom I know personally, by name. That one moved in not long ago and I just haven't seen him or her outside to say, "Hello." Otherwise, Matt and Stefi and the boys often say good morning as they get ready to ride their bikes to school just under one mile across town. That is entirely across town, from one edge to the other. Junie barks at me through the fence posts, looking for a way to get over, under, or around. Then I walk up and over the rise in the road and around the weeping willow on the corner of J Street, where you have to be careful because you cannot see around it, and there is no stop sign in either direction. In the evening, Joe and Jennifer sit on their porch and, with my hand raised up to block the setting sun, I can see them enough to shout a greeting. This is a totally selfish thing, by the way. I

The Root of the Problem

thoroughly enjoy the waves and friendly greetings as I pass by one of many times during any given day.

Mark and his fruit trees live on the right side of the morning commute, just by the turn. The long, narrow side yard that separates the house from the street has become one glorious, fruitful orchard as only a master gardener could produce. There are apples, pears, peaches, and cherries. Underneath bloom spring bulbs in their season, sweet peas in theirs, and rosemary all year long. That cherry tree is a work of art, perfectly manicured for shape and space, leaving the right amount of healthy branches and air in between for a bountiful harvest of fruit. I was walking to the church in the morning while Mark slowly and meticulously pruned those trees. The big straw hat shaded his head and short pants made up his regular off-work uniform. He ascended the ladder, cut precisely, then climbed down again. He stood with his arms crossed and considered the next move. Then the whole process repeated. I stopped and watched for a minute before Mark, with his back to me and intent on the art of the next cut, noticed I was there. I praised his great skill and said my "Have a good day" before heading on to the church to exercise my own craft as the town pastor. Arriving home that evening, I wandered back to my garden where I dragged out a ladder and pair of clippers. My pair of old Corona brand clippers had long since rusted and become so dull that they no longer actually cut all the way through the branch. I put the ladder by the tree and stepped back to consider what my first move should be. Clippers in hand, I tucked my right hand under my left arm, hoping that my two-minute lesson in fruit tree master craft might now flow out of my hands like I actually knew what I was doing. No such luck, unfortunately.

After a few cuts that could be called nothing less than ugly, I returned to the house to lament my inability and found some encouragement from Julie and the kids. But before I passed through the front door, there on the welcome mat rested a small dirt-colored book with orange Post-it tags protruding from several pages, just over halfway through. Mark had dropped it off that day and indicated the pages explaining the best way to prune the fruit trees that I had planted in my yard. Neighbors know what kind of fruit trees you have around here. "How to prune peach and nectarine trees," it said, though it could have been "Peach trees for dummies," for all I knew of the process.

"First, cut out one-year-old branches in the center of the head." So, I did, leaving an open, airy center.

85

"Cut low-hanging branches." So, I did, resulting in a more shapely tree seeming to move upward towards the sun.

"One-year-old twigs; cut back one third." It seems that the best fruit-bearing buds are found on the middle third of one-year-old twigs. I obeyed religiously with the peach tree, followed by the weeping plum, and then blackberries, boysenberries, and gooseberries. They looked magnificent! Not quite up to Mark's quality, but by far the best I had ever done. And the real test came the next spring. Fruit! More peaches than we knew what to do with. I cannot tell you how wonderful that feels and the excitement those little green stones brought to our household. Everyone was out in the yard babying that tree from the first pink flowers until harvest time. We mulched with homegrown compost from our own yard waste and kitchen scraps. We watered deeply, thinned fruit to just three well-spaced specimens, and netted to keep the birds away. Then we picked . . . and picked . . . and picked, easily fifty pounds of the sweetest little donut peaches you have ever tasted. We ate donut peaches by the handfuls. Then we ate donut peach ice cream, drank donut peach smoothies, and spread our toast with donut peach jam. There are still donut peaches in the freezer months later.

The second point in this chapter is like the first: an unhealthy tree needs a good pruning. If you already believe in Jesus but do not live a consistent life from root to fruit, if the people around you and the place where you live are not healthier because you are there, then repent and live into his story of redemption, rescue, and restoration.

Gospel pruning for gospel fruit

In our town, I have been invited to intervene in quarrels over horse corrals. What? That doesn't happen in your town? Sometimes horses don't clean up after themselves, and neighbors suffer the pungent aromas of mounding manure. One time in particular, a lady came to me about her neighbor's corral. "What do I do?" she asked, having lost patience with the situation yet still wanting to be a good neighbor herself. "How do I love my neighbor when I feel like we are at odds?" This is a great question and a situation that involves both people and place.

How do we address the root of this situation? What is at the heart of the matter? The heart of the matter is that these neighbors are divided ,and the land is unkept. The two go together. Well, let's ask ourselves what action is leading to that fruit. In this case, it seems to be the horse owners' failure

The Root of the Problem

to keep the pen clean. But what does the lady coming to me believe that leads her to react in such a way that results in division? Perhaps she feels disrespected, or she assumes that the piled-up manure is a direct gesture against her and her self-worth. This is honestly how we think, or at least, how we respond before we've taken the time to think deeply. Now, how might we preach the gospel to that belief and so bring different fruit?

First, her self-worth is tied to the image of God that she bears and to the redemption that Jesus has brought to her through his great sacrifice. I reminded her of this as our starting point. Even if the manure was malicious, that great worth is not affected in the slightest. The pressure came down immediately. She could address the issue at hand without it becoming a matter of life and death. Second, that neighbor, very likely, had some other part of life simply get in the way. Jesus died for that neighbor, too. Jesus loves that neighbor, too. Jesus wants that neighbor restored and put this woman there to be part of it. That belief will lead to a different action and that different action to different fruit. Anger will lead to further brokenness, but the grace that comes through Jesus restores relationships and gets the mess cleaned up. This is heart change.

You are the root of the ecological problem with your place—your sin and everyone else's along with yours. Sin keeps it from flourishing. Sin requires a Savior, not just a recycling program. But you, as the local church, are a redeemed, restored and recycled people, living restored lives that restore your people and restore your place because the Savior has changed your heart, that you may bear more fruit. This makes creation care a vital local church issue, because the local church is the best place for hard hearts to be renewed and broken people to be restored. There is no other organization under heaven divinely designed for that job but the local church.

Chapter 8

Redeeming and Recycling

We repurposed two wire-framed chairs into garden art. That means we picked them up at a yard sale and stuck them out in the garden. Both the backing and the seats have long since deteriorated, but the rusted structure makes for something beautiful as a trellis for pumpkins or a cage for tomatoes. Pumpkins grow on strong vines and will hang in oblong shapes from the old chairs, even taking the prime seat in the middle space where humans used to sit and rest. Tomatoes don't vine, but they bush out around the chair frame as a support system. Two old wooden ladders have found redemption in a similar way; one guards the round center of garden path planted with herbs. On it, my children have hung the handmade sign that they gave to me for Father's Day: "A man who plants a garden feels as if he has done something good for the world," it reads, reminding me every time I walk the path, picking and trimming as I go. The other disappears into a patch of snap peas every spring as they wind their way up and around the braces and the shelf. These small pieces add a little joy to our lives, and we keeps them from ending up in the landfill. Both the ladders and

Redeeming and Recycling

the chairs came into the family through the same route, the annual Santa Margarita Yard Sale, where a full 10 percent of our town recycles old stuff and the other 90 percent redeems it.

Santa Margarita Beautiful, a group of community leaders, have taken responsibility to get things done around our town, to produce "tangible local benefits," they say. And we join in. Their group is entirely volunteer, which means a whole lot of work that most people never realize goes into their projects. They plan, advertise, schedule, produce maps, and gather sponsors for our trio of spring cleaning events. It begins with an organized cleanup: weed pulling, trash collection, and touch up painting where it is needed. Our place comes back to life a bit through these local hands every April and May. Then there is the scheduled waste pick up and the annual sell-off.

For years, the crew hauled in two enormous white industrial dumpsters from Waste Management to be set up along H Street near the elementary school. Pickup trucks full of neighbors drove in with their junk to be disposed of, and we volunteers unloaded them into the dumpsters while teenagers helped out by jumping up and down on the stuff to get more to fit. Folks dropped off appliances, broken furniture, old hoses ,and two wireframe chairs, redeemed for our garden. Other trucks dropped around town and picked things up for those who had a hard time getting them there, like good Samaritans carrying a neighbor on their donkey. Santa Margarita is neighborly in that way.

They had to stop providing the dumpsters, unfortunately. Waste management would typically place them on the road the night before the pickup day and mysteriously, overnight, stuff would already show up in them without permission. Sometimes they would be full by the time the crew gathered in the park at 8 AM to discuss a plan of attack over coffee. And if someone did not stand guard until the roll-offs were picked up, folks would keep piling garbage up and over the top, even just leaving it on the sidewalks for someone else to worry about. This was not an example of the most neighborly part of town, more like the priest and the levite who passed the hurting neighbor by crossing to the other side of the road. That kind of recycling is not very redeeming.

About sixty homes, out of just over 700 in town, sign up each year to take part in the annual yard sale. The rest come out on foot or on bike to join in the festivities of one of the best days to live in this small town. Cars can't drive down I Street without running over a few hundred pedestrians,

89

God restores people

ambling, shopping, laughing, and catching up. I spend two to three hours just talking, which drives my family absolutely crazy, but how often do you find so many neighbors out front on the same day? The day is about visiting as much as it is about buying and selling. Honestly, how do you haggle with a friend or a neighbor? They are actually trying to get you to take their goods for free by the end of the day, so they don't have to donate them to a local thrift store. If you do buy something, chances are that next year it will show up in your yard sale. The whole town is just recycling.

We load up the bike trailer and head out on our rounds, just like everyone else does. There are lots of bike trailers in Margarita. Some are high quality and store bought—the famous BOB trailers were created in our area. Others are the remnants of old child trailers, now reused with a piece of plywood for a base and a bungee cord to hold it all together. Ours is something in between. We bought something at the yard sale once . . . and used it once. It was a black skimboard with flames painted on it. We paid only $3 and you should have seen me riding around town with it in the trailer. The shoreline is perfect for skimboarding where we live, but my body is not perfect for it. I find that I am not a fan of the hard thud that my old shoulders make when hitting the sand. Last year I went out looking for another old ladder for the garden, but never found one. I mentioned the search to a friend while we were stopped in the middle of the street, and he gave me one that he had in his own garage.

Recycling and redeeming go together for us, just like they do in the story of the Good Samaritan. The team at Santa Margarita Beautiful has created a way in which both people and place can benefit. People get to clean up and a bit and all the stuff is kept out of the local landfill. There are hundreds of ways that people have figured out to do good for both people and place in small ways where they live. Churches can do that too. Your church can be about the business of both redeeming and recycling. You are owned. You are restored. You are sent. You are there. Restored people redeem and recycle; they restore. They live with priest, Levites, Samaritans and a whole host of people whose lives have swerved off into the ditch. They live with those same people in the same place with a different vision, a vision that starts with consistent Christian living from the heart.

Redeeming and Recycling

Redeemed worshippers

Now, we can honestly and finally talk about what to do as God's restored people in the place where we live. You've been trying to get here all along, haven't you? In fact, you probably thought that creation care was simply a matter of what you do or do not do. When we started this conversation, you may have thought that the call to creation care as a local church congregation was going to involve a list of how to make your church building "green". First, you change the light bulbs from energy-wasting incandescent bulbs to incredibly expensive and potentially polluting compact fluorescent types. Many of us think that way, unfortunately. Just like the man who prompted the Good Samaritan story, we seek to justify ourselves by our actions. Jesus was asked a question by a lawyer who was seeking to justify himself. He asked, "What must I do to inherit eternal life?" So, Jesus told him a story that demonstrated how far from the mark we really are. There is no justifying ourselves, no matter how many hurting neighbors we help or how many light bulbs we change. Jesus is the good samaritan. Jesus is the great ecologist. No amount of external actions will change the internal reality. We are sinful at the heart and must be redeemed. Creation care is a call to faith; a call to become whole life disciples; a call to become redeemed worshippers. All of our ecological actions first flow from a heart of faith in something. Ecology is always religious, always the overflow of the heart. Ours is the overflow of a heart that worships, a heart that is justified by faith alone in Christ alone. There is a distinctly Christian approach to ecology. A Christian ecology is simply a whole-life discipleship, following Jesus all the way down to the dirt. Put another way, he owns us, so we worship him as a redeemed people.

Discipleship begins with worship. The first action of restored Christians is to gather as a local church to worship the Savior Jesus, from the heart. Worship itself is learned from the rhythms of creation. Creation worships first. It has always worshipped first, having a good five-day head start on humanity. God created the world to praise him, and it does so naturally. It is we who need to learn to join in the song through redemption. Psalm 148, towards the end of the Psalter where praise is heavy, calls on sun, moon, and stars to exalt the name of the Lord, for he commanded, and they were created. All God's creatures have got a place in the choir, we might say. Then the divine choir director continues the summons,

> Praise the Lord from the earth,

> Sea monsters and all deeps;
>> Fire and hail, snow and clouds;
> Stormy wind, fulfilling His word;
>> Mountains and all hills;
> Fruit trees and all cedars;
>> Beasts and all cattle;
> Creeping things and winged fowl;
>> Kings of the earth and all peoples;
> Princes and all judges of the earth;
>> Both young men and virgins;
> Old men and children.

The mountains and hills praise God. Fruit trees and cattle do too. Stormy wind and snow fulfill his word, it says. Then, and the order matters, kings and princes, young men and children harmonize with creation, note for note. The tune of Christian worship is the song of God's people in harmony with their place.

The heart of worship is shaped and reshaped Sunday after Sunday. Each week God's people come together by command and by desire to worship the one who owns and has a plan for our place. For a couple of hours we stop trying to run the world and take on the great religious task of sitting down, the act which demonstrates more than anything else our faith in God as the owner of the universe and not we ourselves. We stop, sit, rest, and just enjoy all that God is, all that God has done and all that God has given to us. This is the beauty of public worship. This rhythm restores our hearts to God as creatures living in a good creation.

Without Sunday, we never quite manage to get the order right. Without Sunday worship, we just might act out of a belief system inherited from the world. We might start with ourselves because that is how we are shaped to believe and act every day of the week. If you are an irregular church attender, then what you actually do on those off Sundays shapes your heart more than worship, and your people and place will suffer for it. Without the forceful stopping of weekly Sabbath worship, we continue to act as if we own the place and God is serving us. But Sunday worship launches us out into a life of daily worship in our place. Corporate worship is the very rhythm of creation's days, built into it and the purpose of it all. On the seventh day, when all was good, God stopped, sat down, and called the man and the woman to be with him. Yes, the most fundamental ecological action one can take is to go to church.

Redeeming and Recycling

Recycled stewards

The patterns that we practice and the story that we are told on Sunday then lives out in who we are and in what we do as worshippers of God. That is, the worshipping church is about the Great Commission through the local mission. The church is to be about the Great Commandment as well as the Great Commission. Simply put, God owns us and the place, so we worship as redeemed people and we steward the place. We both redeem and recycle.

Peter Harris, founder of A Rocha along with his wife Miranda, has said, "True worship of the living God is the wellspring for sustainable life."[1] That is, ecological sustainability comes from a heart of worship, and, a worshipping heart lives a sustainable life. The church that worships truly will live in its place toward God's ends. Those of you familiar with biblical metaphors are already making the connection between your responsibility to your place, which God owns, and the imagery of a household steward. The steward is the one who runs the house according to the owner's purpose, not his own.

Kathy is the closest thing we have to a steward in our little western town. She met us at the entrance to the old ranch house, where she and her family had lived for over three decades.

"These vines are original mission vines, probably over 200 years old," she told us as we passed underneath the ancient canopied walkway. "That olive is likely original also, but we're not sure."

We stepped up onto the wooden porch that looked just like you would expect the porch to look on a nineteenth-century Wild West ranch house.

"Is that where Patrick Murphy had his picture taken?" I asked, recognizing the steps and gables from the old picture of the Santa Margarita Ranch's second owner during a fiesta.

"It is, and doesn't it look exactly the same?" She was right; it looked exactly the same.

We entered through the door and into the kitchen, which, she says, was added on some years ago because the original kitchen was its own outbuilding, as was common for the time. Passing from the kitchen, it became obvious that we stepped back in time. We stepped through the thick adobe walls and into the original house. There were several main rooms that each faced the direction of the porch and bedrooms branched off in the other directions. But it was the walls that made the place feel old, because they

---

1. Harris, *Kingfisher's Fire*, 152.

were old. They were old and yet entirely maintained. We stood there with Kathy, listening to her stories of what had transpired in those rooms and could feel the well-preserved history that still lived in that house with her.

The Estrada Adobe, named after Joaquin Estrada who first received title to the Queen of the Ranchos in the 1840s, had been occupied consistently until just a few years ago. Kathy stewarded the property well. Kathy preserved and embodied the history of our town in both her heart and in that house. Our entire town has benefited from Kathy's stewardship and we are grateful to her.

Perhaps these few good biblical stories will help with what it means to be a steward. Do you remember Joseph, the favored son of the patriarch Jacob with the Technicolor dream coat? Joseph had dreams about the day when his brothers (and his parents!) would bow down to him like he was the sun itself and they the moon and the stars. After he, foolishly, told the brothers about the dream, they sold him into slavery, which is about as far from bowing down to him as you can get. In spite of the evil intentions of those jealous brothers, God intended that Joseph would become the ideal steward in a household belonging to the King of Egypt. Pharaoh held nothing back from Joseph: "Only as regards the throne will I be greater than you," he said. Pharaoh gave him free use of all things because he knew that Joseph would use it the way that Pharaoh intended (Gen 41:40). And, yes, eventually his brothers did bow down to him, and when they did, he restored them. When we say we are stewards in God's house, we mean we are like Joseph was to Pharaoh, to the land, and to his brothers. God has given us dominion under his dominion. Yet, in regards to the throne, he will always be greater than us. We steward well when the wheat harvest is managed well and the people are fed. We steward well when those who have sinned against us are forgiven and redeemed.

Then there is the story of a faithful and sensible steward Jesus told in the Gospel according to Luke, chapter 12. He is a "wise manager whom his master will set over his household . . . . Blessed is that servant whom his master will find so doing when he comes . . . . And that servant who knew his master's will but did not get ready or act according to his will, will receive a severe beating" (Luke 12:42–48). We are the faithful and sensible stewards who have been given much in God's house. And we will be held accountable to act accordingly in both his church and in the people and the place the church has been sent to with both a commission and a

Redeeming and Recycling

commandment, to preach the gospel of forgiveness in Jesus, and to restore by great acts of love.

The Apostle Paul insists that he be understood as one thing and no more. He calls himself a steward in the household of God. "Moreover, it is required of stewards that they be found faithful" (1 Cor 4:2). Think of all the ways Paul could have defined himself: Apostle! Scholar! Miracle worker! Martyr! Paul had a resumé that most people only dream about. But Paul loved this identity because it fit so well. It is what every Christian is, no matter when or where we live. We are stewards of God in our place. This is the one word on our Christian business card. That is our one job description.

Do you hear it? Are you making the connection? Joseph was God's steward in Egypt; Paul was God's steward of God's gospel to the Gentile people of the world, and *you are God's steward where you live*. It is required of stewards that they are found faithful to the owner of the house. Your place is God's place. You are God's stewards in his ecological house, the place where you live. Wendell Berry once wrote, "It is not allowable to love the creation according to the purposes one has for it any more than it is allowable to love one's neighbor in order to borrow his tools."[2]

The one who loves God, who worships God, does so not just to borrow his tools. The one who loves God will love God's tools: God's creation, God's people, and God's place. There is no need to try to separate them and they cannot honestly be separated. The church that loves and worships truly will make disciples who both redeem and recycle.

Psalm 148 was the theme passage for year three of Creation Care Camp. Our children looked deeply at the plants and bugs and animals that thrive in their place and learned to join in the praise. They discovered what it means for each to flourish, as God created them to, and how our participation either helps or hinders them. They saw the divine beauty that when creation flourishes, we have more to love. In the morning Bible lesson, we sat them down under the trees on canvas tarps just outside the fence of the Santa Margarita Elementary School garden. Benjamin led us all in singing the camp theme song, "God Made Them All," written by the ladies in Rain for Roots. We read Psalm 148, focusing on verse 10: "[Praise the Lord] Beasts and all cattle; Creeping things and winged fowl."

"How do the animals praise?" we asked. The answer is by fulfilling their purpose, by filling their place in creation. There is no other end

---

2. Berry, *The Gift of Good Land*, 273.

needed; they do not need to be of any practical use to us in order to praise God. God created the animals for himself to enjoy. They praise him just by being there, by doing what they do. And they point our sights beyond themselves to the one who created them. After the lesson, we sent the children out to see how the animals flourish, goats in particular—goats matter in Santa Margarita.

They played goat-themed field games, running from corner to corner, matching feed with goats as David and Kelsey hollered out clues. Jim and Jill from Hollyhock Hollow brought out a few samples of their herd of Pygora goats. Jim and Jill are good friends and a intricate part of our little town, Jim as a part of the Santa Margarita Lions Club and Jill as a part of, well, everything. Pygoras are a breed developed by crossing the smaller Pygmy goats with Angora, which produce large quantities of quality fleece. Our children fed, touched, and smelled two kids and two mature goats.

"Are they same kind of animal?" one wee one asked our visiting rancher. They really did look significantly different. The mature set had longer hair and were wider by multiples and larger by inches at the withers.

"What's that on the ground all around them?" inquired another, eliciting giggles from the older, though maybe not more mature, children as they pointed out the raisin-like droppings already piling up around the portable fencing.

Jim and Jill brought samples of that magnificent Pygora fleece and other neighbors taught the children to spin wool from goat hair. To cap it all off, they ate goat cheese for a snack. Fleece and cheese are just two ways that the children literally found joy in good care of the goats—as the goats flourished, so did the children.

At the end of the day, we brought the children back together, read the psalm to them one more time, and asked what they noticed about the animals of our place. "How were they wise, showing us that God is wise? How were they powerful, showing us that God is powerful? How were they beautiful, showing that God is beautiful?" And the children answered because goat memories were as fresh in their minds as the goat smell on their clothes.

"God enjoys the animals he created to praise him. God gives them breath and food every day. You can praise him with every breath too," we taught them, making the biblical connection clear for them, now that they had tangibly experienced God's goats in their place. "Did you enjoy the animals? Do you believe in Jesus today as the animals have taught you?" It is easy to get from goats to Jesus ... and, yes, we did tell them that in the Bible it is better to be a sheep than a goat.

These children are becoming disciples who both redeem and recycle. Like Joel Salatin—that Christian, libertarian, environmentalist, lunatic farmer—they are in the redemption business. Joel describes the mission of his PolyFace Farms in Virginia's Shenandoah Valley this way: "We are in the redemption business: healing the land, healing the food, healing the economy, and healing the culture." We are in the redemption business, too. In the church, we call it discipleship, and discipleship goes all the way down to the dirt.

But we must redeem and not just recycle

If all ecology is an act of worship, how do we avoid falling into the paganism of fear and guilt? We often feel like we have to put up our fists to fight because we refuse to enter into the religious habits of much of the environmental movement. Or we may just feel so pummeled by the constant moral outrage leveled against us as a human destructive force that we give in and install a low-flow toilet. We end up making token efforts based on sentimentality rather than truth, and that cannot truly restore. This is a very real conflict for Christians in creation care today, especially in the US, where people and place have been separated into two distinct political issues. The ecological green religion often has Christians bound up, not knowing what to do that would not violate a firm faith in Jesus who puts heaven and earth, people and place, back together. What pastoral guidance might we offer?

First, do not fear. We worship the one true God who created all things, owns all things, and is reconciling all things to himself. As we've already said, a recycling program cannot undo what Jesus has already accomplished in redemption.

Second, be consistent with your own world view. We sometimes do not act because we don't want to act like "them." Fine. Just be consistent with your faith in the incarnate, sacrificed, and risen Christ. You pray daily, "your kingdom come, your will be done." You believe that God has already begun the restoration of this broken world when he stepped out of the tomb on Easter Sunday. So, continually ask what God intends for the people and place where you dwell. Continue to ask what the fruit of resurrection life would be and then act towards that end. It does not have to be achieved in

God restores people

total for real practical good to come about. Do that practical, tangible good; do your recycling.

Third, help your unbelieving neighbors see the glory of the gospel lived out in the way you bring restoration, both redeeming sinners and renewing places. Help them to see that they are actually acting inconsistently themselves because they have no reason to seek the restoration of either people or place without a belief in Jesus as the redeemer of broken people and broken world.

C. S. Lewis may have considered the paganism of today's environmental movement to be good news for the local church. Pagans who worship the earth are closer to a faith in Jesus than most modern men because they already believe something, and they already worship something. Their ecology is an act of faith, and that means our efforts at recycling, creation care, open wonderful doors to the gospel that matters so much to us. At one point, Lewis calls pagans "imminently convert-able."

> I sometimes wonder if we will have to re-convert men to real paganism as a preliminary converting them to Christianity. If they were Stoics, Orphics, Mithraists, or (better still) peasants worshipping the Earth, our task might be easier. This is why I don't consider contemporary Paganism as a wholly bad symptom.[3]

Perhaps this is a time when recycling might lead to redemption because we learn to live as God's restored people in all of the places where God has put a local church. Perhaps this is a time when the world can see that the only consistent way to care for creation is to worship the creator God. But we cannot run away; we cannot disengage. Those who worship differently, whether they worship the earth as pagans, the all sovereign self or idols, either carved statues or the idols of the heart, all seek to justify themselves like the Good Samaritan's lawyer. They all need redemption in Jesus who offers free justification by faith alone. And so does the planet that is suffering because of it.

Worship and stewardship fit together nicely, like redeeming and recycling. But what kind of life is consistent with belief in the one true God? What kind of life works towards God's end? What kind of life actually puts people and place back together?

---

3. Lewis, *Present Concerns*, 66.

Chapter 9

Just Plant Onions

The other day I realized that I have never discovered a new species and felt kind of bad about that. Of course, I knew that already. You usually know when you have discovered a new species. That is not one of those things that you just stumble on. "Oops, I think I discovered a new species. Perhaps I should tell someone. Perhaps I should be more careful where I am stepping." I have never identified a previously unknown spider, frog, or plant and probably never will. Being a part of the work of A Rocha can make you feel like an inadequate environmentalist, don't you know. I mean, while our brothers and sisters were tromping unexplored forests in Papua New Guinea, I was planting a fall garden in my California backyard.

My fall garden is so very different than my spring and summer garden. In summer, she runneth over with green, overcoming her raised-bed boundaries like an adolescent whose arms are bigger than she realizes. Fall is much simpler, much tidier. The beds have been cleaned of the frost-killed summer veg, packed down with compost mixed together from yard and kitchen scraps, chicken droppings and the leftovers from my neighbor's horse corral. My nine beautiful boxes shine with fresh yellow straw and just a few, very precisely placed fall plantings: cabbage, broccoli, red spotted heirloom romaine, beets, and some amazing torpedo onion sprouts that my neighbor swears will grow better in our microclimate than any bulbs I could buy at the store.

Years ago, I planted standard red onion bulbs purchased in bulk at a locally owned hardware store. They started out as these gorgeous little baby onions, so tender and in need of my fatherly care. I put them to bed at a good time and nurtured them kindly as they rested for the winter, giving them a drink whenever they cried about being thirsty. And in the spring I harvested . . . flowers, not onions. They were not even an undiscovered flower, just onion flowers. Having provided the neighborhood with a good laugh at my expense, I was let in on the secret: in our climate zone, we need to use torpedo onion starts, rather than bulbs for planting. "Starts" are onion plants that are put into the ground after they are a few months along.

One afternoon I got a phone call. Hoping it might be from an A Rocha colleague in need of my species-discovering help, I answered in my most scientific voice. The call wasn't from Papua New Guinea. It was, however, a neighbor informing me of the time and place I could acquire "the" onions. I headed out to his house and returned home with my little package of wet, newspaper-wrapped sprouts. Now in the ground, my starts look pretty good so far. My parenting routine begins again. We'll have to wait until spring before we know if this is the species that will flourish in my neighborhood. But I have it on the best local authority (aka town gossip) that it is.

Why do I care so about such things? Peter Harris says this about the work of discovering new species: "We are motivated by our conviction that every species matters because it is part of God's good creation, whether or not it has obvious value for humans . . . . When a species is wiped out . . . we are removing a member of the choir."[1]

Peter's words apply to all of us as we seek to live faithfully in God's world. I am not a biologist, geologist, ornithologist, or zoologist, and I have never discovered a new species. I am an ordinary local church pastor who is discovering ways in which I can live day to day under the Lordship of Christ for whom, by whom, and through whom all things were created and all things hold together—whether frogs and spiders in Papua New Guinea or onions in my backyard. How do we live a life as God's restored people,

---

4. Harris, *A Rocha International Newsletter*.

sent to restore both people and place? Just plant onions, but plant the right onions for your place.

Planting onions is creation care. Planting the right kind of onions is the kind of life that flows from worship. It is not a new program or a Christian version of "greening" your life. It is just simple Christian living that fits your place. It is living that is free because the grace of Jesus Christ has set us free from the sin of that old paganism and its consequences; it is living that allows us to be at home in the world because we people belong here as much as the animals and because Jesus was born into this world to make us and it new, even now; and it is living that is full of hope because we know that through preaching and living, God's restored people can and do restore people and places, not perfectly of course, but truly nonetheless. We know that one day God will make all things right.

Live like he has set you free

Freedom is not a word that we associate with environmentalism today. Who read the United Nations report on climate change and said, "I feel so much more free and joyful?" (As if anyone actually read the report.) But Christians in creation care are free because of the grace of Jesus. In a *Christianity Today* interview with Eugene Peterson and Peter Harris, Harris noted,

> Recently a social scientist at the Cornell Lab of Ornithology told me that studies have shown one of the marker personality traits among environmentalists is anxiety. The Christian approach is very different: it is celebratory and grateful and hopeful.[2]

We are now free to live joyfully because God owns the place, and we are his stewards. God created the world out of the overflow of his happiness. It is fallen, yes, but you have been redeemed through faith in Jesus, and all things are being reconciled to God in Christ. Therefore, life in this world can be good and joyous because the earth is good and joyous.

Biblical freedom is the grand gift of God's goodness in a broken world. We are free in Christ Jesus, free from the power of sin to force us into destructive actions and free from sin's destructive consequences. We are free from the bonds of sin and death. The grace of God that has set us free is true freedom, freedom to live a new life even in this world as it is today.

2. Crouch, "The Joyful Environmentalists."

God restores people

Both are true at the same time: you are free in Christ and this world needs restoration. Hold them to be true at the same time. The freedom that comes from the God who owns everything is the freedom to do all the possible good that he planned when he created the place. And the coming of Jesus has made it even clearer. You are free to live abundantly where you live.

When we feel hindered and overwhelmed by conversations about wholistic discipleship and creation care, it is usually because we are worshiping wrongly and it is resulting in a pagan legalism, not a Christian freedom. The inherited faith of environmentalism as a religion causes the brokenness of the present world to overshadow the freedom of grace in Jesus.

Much of the environmental movement confesses a fear- and guilt-based religion: "The world will end if you drive another mile!" As A Rocha's Dave Timmer has written so beautifully, "Environmental legalism is still legalism." He goes on to say, "Creation care is so much more than taking the reusable tote to the grocery store, changing light bulbs, or eating organic produce. It is so much more than even giving everything we own to the poor. It is following Jesus. Creation care is reaching to grasp what God is doing in the places where we live."[3]

Freedom is the exact opposite of piling burdens onto your already busy shoulders. Jesus warns of those hypocritical Pharisees who tie up heavy burdens and lay them on people's shoulders, but they themselves are unwilling to move them with so much as a finger (Matt. 23:4). Beware of environmental Pharisees! The burdens caused by a new set of ecological rules is the same kind of moral legalism and it is deadly, not freeing.

In that *Christianity Today* interview, the final question posed Peterson and Harris was this: "Clearly there is a growing enthusiasm among Christians for creation care. But enthusiasm can go wrong. What do you see as the deepest risks in our current interest in environmental concerns?" Peter Harris responded:

> I think eco-judgmentalism is a real danger. This is not a matter of finding another five quick rules to keep you on the right side of God. This is not about what we do; this is a change or a development in the depth of our relationship with God himself. It's about everything, not just about a narrow slice of topics. It would be disastrous if we turn the biblical vision into a code that "good" Christians follow—something like, thou shalt eat muesli, wear sandals, and look miserable. I think the environmental movement

3. Timmer, "Beyond the 'Green' Commandments."

Just Plant Onions

has been perceived as judgmental and angry, claiming moral high ground and issuing rules with disapproval.[4]

The Christian call to creation care, a thoroughly Christian ecology, is one of freedom, not a series new of Levitical laws about dirt, animals, and food.

They say that food has replaced sex as the new moral code. Fifty years after the sexual revolution the only thing immoral about sexuality is to suggest that there is a moral attached to sexuality. Marriages are in decline while cohabitation is on the rise, even among younger Christians. They are "sexual atheists," one commentator has said; they believe that Jesus is their Savior, but they don't believe Jesus has a clue about sex. Children are increasingly raised by single-parent families, and even intact families have lost any moral language for talking about sex and gender. It is considered taboo, even oppressive, to suggest that sex might be taboo outside of marriage, as the Bible teaches. No, today the moral language is reserved for what we eat.

Mary Eberstadt of Stanford University's Hoover Institution has made comparisons with the behaviors of some people today in regards to food and those of previous generations in regards to sex. She sees them changing rapidly and in an inverse relationship.

> Unable or unwilling (or both) to impose rules on sex at a time when it is easier to pursue it than ever before, yet equally unwilling to dispense altogether with a universal moral code that he would have bind society against the problems created by exactly that pursuit, modern man (and woman) has apparently performed his own act of transubstantiation. He has taken longstanding morality about sex, and substituted it onto food. The all-you-can-eat buffet is now stigmatized; the sexual smorgasbord is not.[5]

Human beings will always have a moral code. We are moral animals. Food and eating may be the cause of new guilt, but not for the Christian who is free in Christ.

In a series of articles titled "Food is the New Sex," Anglican Pastor Aaron Damiani acknowledges that the talk about food in his Chicago congregation can be "moral" in both tone and word choice. He carefully suggests that it is wise to consider that food and eating are both actually ethical acts. The answer to food legalism is not to deny that eating is ethical. Of

---

4. Crouch, "The Joyful Environmentalists."
5. Eberstadt, "Is Food the New Sex?"

God restores people

course it is; food and eating are ethical in relation to both God and others throughout the Bible.

Adam and Eve are fed and work as gardeners with God in the beginning. In fact, things begin to go wrong when they eat with the wrong person. Noah is given all things to eat after the flood in remembrance that life comes from the mercy of God. That mercy is more clearly seen in the eating of the Passover meal and then the eating of the last supper with Jesus, which Christians commemorate with bread and wine at Communion.

There are also the ethics of growing food and feeding the poor in the Bible. Levitical laws insist that believing farmers leave portions of their fields for the poor to glean. Others demand a giving of a tithe every three years for the sake of the poor. And, one day, God's restored people of every place will sit down in God's restored place to eat the marriage supper of the lamb. So, yes, both growing food and eating food are ethical acts. There is a universal moral code that is involved. But how can we apply this code biblically rather than the new pagan moralism?

Damiani suggests several ways in which clergy can wisely shepherd both the foodie "elder brothers" and foodie "younger brothers," as he calls them.

> I believe the new food righteousness has produced both "elder siblings" and "younger siblings," both of whom may be in our congregations or spheres of influence. The elder siblings are those who put their hope in food-righteous, however they define it. This morality code has made them smug, neurotic, or both. When the opportunity presents itself, we can warn the food-pious among us of the temptation to engage in self-righteous shaming and tongue-clucking at those who fall short.... Younger siblings, on the other hand, are in a state of rebellion against the new food asceticism. I would posit that this is a populous group.... When people are shamed, especially about their diet, they often react with defiance and anger. A wise shepherd can help them identify their anger and teach them how to respond in the way of Jesus. Ultimately, both elder siblings and younger siblings need to transact with the grace of God, which promises to heal and set in order our relationship with food.[6]

Whether it is entirely true that the world of universal moral codes has shifted, it may be too early to tell, but the food struggle is real wherever

---

6. Damiani, "Food is the New Sex."

food growers and food eaters live in the same community. Damiani sees that in his congregation and so do I.

In our town, we have both sides of this food-growing conversation. We've got ranchers, and we've got vineyard owners. We've got industrial farmers, and we've got organic farmers. We've got restauranteurs who purchase their food from restaurant supply stores and we've got others who only buy from farms where they know both the soil and the farmer. It would be simple to condemn one another and to walk away. We are learning to live together, to grow food together, to eat together with freedom because of Jesus. We are learning to have substantial conversations for restoration because we are God's people in this place. We actually have the grounds for freedom, not more guilt. Damiani offers wisdom for those involved in food supply.

> We can commission those in the food industry to carry out the creation mandate. When God blessed man and woman and invited them to rule the earth under his authority, he specifically mentions the food supply: "Behold, I have given you every plant yielding seed that is on the face of the earth, and every tree ... you shall have them for food" (Gen 1:29–30). Food is fundamental to our care for and interaction with God's creation. Many of us minister among those who steward the earth's food supply through their work in restaurants, farms, meat-packing facilities, food distribution centers, and Community Supported Agriculture. We can affirm the employees and owners of these establishments that the food industry and their work within it matters to God, and encourage them to pursue justice and the common good through their work.[7]

Think about your actual neighborhood for a moment. It has boundaries that mark off where it stops being your neighborhood and becomes someone else's neighborhood. That is good. Limitations are good. Accept your limitations for now and let's talk about being disciples right there. Really, who can be responsible for the whole world at once? Where might the false guilt of environmentalism without God need the message of the free grace of Jesus through you?

If your neighborhood is anything like mine, then you live in a house of some sort on a piece of ground of some sort. You might have neighbors with similar configurations pretty close to you. Both that ground and that

---

7. Ibid.

house require cultivating and keeping. You are already doing cultivating. Is it an act of worship? Do you mow the lawn as if it is God's lawn? Do you love your neighbors in the way you mow, the time of morning you mow, and in what kind of fertilizer you put on the grass? Once you have a vision of what it would look like for your neighborhood to flourish, then you can start making small decisions towards that end because you love and worship the God who owns it and placed you there to care for it. Making small decisions concerning your home water run-off will directly affect your neighbors. Making small decisions concerning whom you buy your food from, can impact a very particular family who grows that broccoli in your area. Make small decisions to spend time cleaning a neighborhood lot that has been neglected, or small decisions planting a garden in unused space for both beauty and nourishment make a difference.

How is it possible for brothers and sisters to carry out some of these things in a suburban neighborhood when they don't know their neighbors, where their water comes from, or where it goes to when it runs off the lawn? Here is my honest answer at this stage of my pastoral life: I don't think you can. This does not mean that you are off the hook for care for God's creation; it means that you are on the hook for knowing your neighbors, where your water comes from, and where it is going. You cannot make any informed choices without knowing. You cannot love without knowing. You cannot be a disciple of Jesus to either people or place without first knowing your people and your place. Maybe that is where this all needs to start for you. First, repent of not loving your neighbors or your place enough to know them. Then look out at them with the grace, faith, and freedom that comes from Christ.

Living with God's joyous freedom will bring about more good where you live than could ever come from the fear and despair caused by the preaching of imminent doom. Believe God, not the doomsday prophets. The first thing you must do is to relax; you have the right starting point. Worshipping God is the right starting point. Then just try redirecting a few small things that are already part of your day-to-day life in light of your new freedom.

Live like this is home

Soon after the spring storms stop breaking over the Cuesta Pass for the season, we head out for the Santa Margarita Beautiful cleanup day. We

Just Plant Onions

serve our older neighbors by cleaning up their yards and making minor repairs, we paint the downtown benches and pull weeds in the Santa Margarita Demonstration Forest, a human-designed patch of trees educating our children about the trees that grow here naturally, though maybe not all in the same grove the way we have them ordered. As my family and I struggled one year to free the magnificent native plants from the encroachment of invading grasses, I remembered something true and important. Since the fall of Adam and Eve in the original garden, the natural tendency of all things earthly is toward weeds and thorns.

If we just let it go, the world would end up covered in Star Thistle and Kudzu. No, we have a part in these things! We have a part in keeping weeds at bay and in cultivating the place toward flourishing as God intended. Humans are not unnatural! You belong here. This world is your home until either you die or until Jesus returns and things are renewed. We tend to treat our homes well. We keep our homes clean, even if just in the spring. We make the necessary repairs to our homes so that the roof doesn't leak or the plumbing fail, and we manage our property towards a greater good. It is an unloving Christian who keeps an ugly lawn that their neighbors have to look at everyday.

Cows are in my blood and sometimes in my backyard when they break through the fence protecting my garden from the neighboring ranch land. My cultivated hollyhocks must taste better than the wild chicory. We have cattle because we have grassland. Grasses grow better than torpedo onion starts. For example, the Carrizo Plain National Monument, a 200,000-acre preserve of California grassland reached by passing through Santa Margarita from the west, keeps a twenty-four-page list of native plants that grow in their area of responsibility. The Bureau of Land Management hires local ranchers to bring cattle on the monument early in the season to preserve and protect native habitat. Cattle graze off the nonnative grasses that emerge early and then are removed to allow the natives to flourish later in the season. The aim is to increase native plant populations, and at the same time to protect endangered species that could potentially be damaged by overgrazing. The people, who belong here, engage the cattle to help care for the place and that home-like management restores both the people and the place.

My great-grandfather, Carey B. Jameson, ranched cattle as most early settlers did in Texas. He raised short Durham, to be precise, and a few Rambouillet sheep. My great-grandfather raised the cattle, and my grandfather processed them. That, if you don't know, is a euphemism for the hard and messy work of slaughtering the animal for food. Our theology of eating always includes death. Whenever we eat, we remember that we only live because there was a death in substitute. That is why we give thanks at mealtime. It is a sobering moment of the day to bow our heads together around the dinner table. Remember Psalm 104: in the poem, God waters the mountains and causes the water to gather into streams that wind their way down to the plains where they water the grasses for the cows to eat. Then the poem turns to include us in the system because we belong there. What does humanity do in the psalm? It labors. You are a part of the place. It is your home as much as it is home to the cows. Treating your place like home will make it better for you, for your neighbor, and for the cows.

Some of you don't have cows on your property. Some of you don't have property. Some of you actually have sidewalks. Some of you commute to work. Unfortunately, there is no psalm written about commuters. But there could be. What does it look like to be at home when your version of home includes a thirty-minute drive to your workplace? That will be a good topic to discuss as a congregation who actually lives there, who makes that place home.

Live like you have hope

We still have not said much about what to do. No one can answer that question without living in a place, without first making it home. We have said that the grace of Jesus has given you freedom to live like that place is home. Settle down. Enjoy it. The hope is that if your heart and mind are changed about your place in God's world, then grace and freedom will lead to find the particulars to work on. You will search for the kind of onions that grow in your climate.

In Dave's neighborhood up in northwest Washington, a long history of land modifications has had a real impact on the place as it is today. Ditching creeks, draining wetlands, and clearing the forest have made way for working dairy farms. This is the physical reality in which they are living and in which they have to work together as a community to bring health. It will not do to either demonize those who have gone before or to romanticize a Henry David Thoreau kind of wilderness. No, people belong there and modifying can be just another word for cultivating. Hope modifies for the

Just Plant Onions

long term, so that the place is good for generations of people and the people are good for the place.

In that real context, a community of people, a community of sinners, will have to address their own hearts, change the way they think, and become more whole disciples together if their place is to be transformed and become healthy once again. Through Dave, A Rocha, and the local churches, that conversation is taking place, and it is turning into real local action.

The pagan religious fear of much of the secular environmental movement is not needed to restore people and places and is not adequate for solving the actual problem. Every action happens within a story, defines a problem, banks its hope on some form of redemption, and then establishes a set of actions consistent with that religious belief. All environmental action is religious action. Without God, who restores all things, there is no offer of hope, only fear for the future. A distinctly Christian ecology offers hope most adequately because it is true to the way things actually are in world, where creation is both good and fallen. And it gives the good hope that the way things are right now—think the worst that you know of, polluted, past the carbon threshold, without common morality, wars and rumors of wars—the way things are right now is not the way things have to be.

Here is why you can have hope, because Jesus has been resurrected and because he will make all things new. Your God became a human, like you, lived in a real place, like yours. He died a sacrificial death, his dust and breath died . . . and that same dust came to life again. The breath of the Holy Spirit was breathed back into Jesus, and he stepped out of his grave to launch the redemption of it all, not the destruction of it all. The resurrection body of Jesus is the firstfruits of the resurrection of us all. The resurrection promises a good future for all of creation that groans for the day when the sons and daughters of God will be revealed. Jesus has been raised from the dead, so you must have hope. And not just hope for your personal redemption, that glorious day when your body and soul will once again be made perfect together, but for the redemption of all things. On that day, Jesus will glorify all who believe by uniting our renewed souls with our resurrected bodies—and he will place us in the new heaven and new earth where there is a new garden, a new river, and a new tree of life whose leaves will be for the healing of the nations.

When God created all things good, he also put into it a created purpose to bring about good, and he intends that it will *one day* achieve that end in spite of the brokenness that we inflict on our world everyday. Right now, our world is not as it should be! But it can be redeemed. One day, Jesus will return. One day, Jesus will judge all things justly, and we will be satisfied. One day, Jesus will make all things right! People and place will be put back together. You must have hope.

This redemption is what Christians call the "good news." God himself has entered into his created world in order to take the brokenness and wrong seriously and to put the pieces back together. Jesus is the only true ecologist, the only one truly at home in the world. He lived in light of God's story, assessed the problem rightly as being rooted in the heart of mankind. He sacrificed himself in order to set things right by forgiving our true guilt, carrying away our real shame, and removing the need we have to blame one another personally, governmentally, or corporately. In calling the people in our place to "follow him," we not only enable them to find forgiveness, but we give them the hope that restores.

We cannot expect to actually restore the world, can we?

Some will inevitably push back at this saying, "We cannot expect to actually restore the world, can we?" No, we cannot expect that. Final restoration will only take place when Jesus returns, not from our creation care efforts, even if those efforts are grounded in freedom and hope. However, that is not really relevant to the task at hand. Even if we cannot restore people and place entirely, we can still restore them substantially. Just as we do not worry about completely evangelizing the world before we find value in evangelizing our neighbors. Do what you can and you will actually find that evangelism and ecology go hand in hand. Your neighbors will see your good works and the good will that results will open doors for the good news.

Live in the hope that God's redemption in Jesus has restored us and then join him in restoring the world, its people, and its places. Do not start a program; just plant the right onions.

God's restored people restore people and places

The people restored by the gospel, saved from sin by the Savior, are prepared, placed, and organized to join in the work of restoration. God's people are in the business of both redemption and recycling, putting people and place back together. God's people restoring people, through great commission preaching, and places, through great commandment loving, are what we call a local church.

Chapter 10

You Are There

I sat down at a dinner table with Ken Wytsma at the Laity Lodge on the Frio River in the hill country of Texas. A Rocha had sponsored an event featuring Eugene Peterson and Peter Harris, "Creation, Community and the Church." Ken and I both attended and ended up at one of those special dinner tables served up with southern hospitality the way that only the Laity Lodge could provide. Entering the Lodge dining room is like entering a southern lady's kitchen. The tables are spread to promote conversation and the food served family style. You have to actually say, "Pass the potatoes please" and get talking to the person sitting next to you. They set out a platter of brownies just like my Grandma Opal used to make, made with light-colored baking cocoa and margarine to get that crisp crust and sharp corners. I ran into the kitchen with a little too much enthusiasm considering they were still serving a meal to 150 guests. "These brownies taste just like my Grandma used to make." Brownies in California are just not the same. Tim and his kitchen staff entered into my joy and sent me home with the recipe. My wife had to ask what oleo was—seems that it's a Texas

God's restored people restore people and places

thing. Ken and I begin to speak, and in just a moment, I knew I wanted to hear more. Ken pastors Antioch Church in Bend, Oregon, and founded the Justice Conference. He told the story of how one church in central Oregon began to gather Christians involved in justice causes around the world. He said that when a church grows to a certain size, traditional wisdom says to plant a new church fifteen minutes away. However, fifteen minutes away from Bend is a whole lot of nothing. So they began to ask what they might do for the world and the Justice Conference was born. You can read more of Ken's story and the Justice Conference story in his book *Pursuing Justice*.

It would be an understatement to say that Ken inspired me. Our church is as much smaller than Antioch Church, as Santa Margarita is than Bend. There is a size of growth in a local church that is just obnoxious in a small town, so there will be a day when we will stop growing either naturally or intentionally. Instead of asking what conference we should be starting, we began asking how we might bring restoration more deeply to the people and place of Santa Margarita. Is there another layer that we can overlay on the map and bring greater good to this place? We seek to bring redemption to our people through corporate worship, making disciples, and reaching out with the gospel. We've added one layer to the map and we seek to bring restoration to the land that our people live on. We do this teaching our disciples to live wholly (starting with our children), by getting our hands dirty where we can, and by partnering with other organizations who are caring for the land in our place. This is our job as a local church. We are God's restored people locally organized to restore our local people and our local places. But what other layers can we add? Is there a way we can increase the voice we have as a gospel witness in this place? How might we organize the church members to do more consistent, strategic, and long-term good for our neighbors, their children, and grandchildren? Is there a way we can help relieve poverty in our town in an organized way? Who is doing that work already? Can we join them? We are still asking many of these questions.

I love this place, if that has not become obvious. I love its characters and its characteristics. These are my neighbors, my friends, and our lives are interconnected. Even more, I am different because of them. I am better because of them. My mother reminds me to be grateful because these people and this place have both given me a home and continued to allow me to grow. Permission to grow is not something that a pastor is afforded very often. I am blessed to belong to Santa Margarita and its people 125 years after its founding on that April day in 1889. I want to serve them with everything that is in me for all the days I have left in this life. I hope and pray that both are better when I leave than when I arrived.

What about your place? What is that next layer that your church can set over the map and bring restoration? In their helpful book, *What Every Pastor Should Know: 101 Indispensable Rules of Thumb for Leading Your Church*, Gary L. MacIntosh and Charles Arn call projects like these "side doors" to your church. See these as an integral part of loving your community, as a part of your local outreach. No one can tell you what to do next who does not live in that place, but there is some guidance that can come from what A Rocha has learned over thirty years. A Rocha projects, wherever they are found around the world, are all characterized by five core commitments. Let these categories guide you in discerning the real and tangible ways your local church might engage in the restoration of your people and your place. People and place really do go together, and God wants you to restore them both.

Christian

Underlying all we do is our biblical faith in the living God, who made the world, loves it, and entrusts it to the care of human society. Our Christian faith is the foundation and motivation for all we seek to be and do. In caring for creation we are responding to the biblical revelation of one living God—Father, Son, and Holy Spirit. God is present and active in his world as creator, sustainer, and redeemer, and calls people to act as responsible stewards of the earth. Our relationship with God enables us to integrate concern for sustainable human and non-human communities in practical expressions of Christian faith, hope, and love in a fragmented world.

If you do not know how to truly connect your Christian theology with you creation care actions, you will act based upon what you have learned from your culture. Most younger people today have a default leaning towards environmental concerns, having been raised in a world in which the effects of our choices are widely known. But if we are not acting from a Christian ecology, then even attempts at good actions will be ultimately destructive. Only gospel actions can restore because only the gospel solves the true problem in our world.

What does that mean for you? It means you must learn and you must teach and that takes time, but the time is worth it. If you do not hold a

God's restored people restore people and places

consistently Christian view of the world, starting with God and working toward God's ends, then it can never be passed on to another generation, and this work of restoration needs the cooperation of many generations. A little learning will enable your actions to last for lifetimes. You have already started this process with this book. Perhaps now you can read it again with others, all the while asking, "Where does God wish to bring restoration to our place?"

Here are just a few other resources you might find helpful. These are all accessible writings that any Christian believer would do well to read alone or with a group. See the bibliography for a longer list of resources.

- *The Radical Disciple*, by John Stott.
- *Under the Bright Wings*, by Peter Harris.
- *Planted: Stories of Creation, Calling and Community*, by Leah Kostamo.
- *Planetwise*, by Dave Bookless.
- *Serve God, Save the Planet*, by J. Matthew Sleeth, MD.

There is no need to wait to act until you have learned, but the learning must take place. You and your church, more deeply restored, is the best action you can take in the work of restoration.

Conservation

We carry out research for the conservation and restoration of the natural world and run environmental education programs for people of all ages. Within the vast range of environmental and ecological concerns that exist today, A Rocha's prime focus is nature conservation. This concern is expressed by the protection of important habitats and species and by the restoration of degraded habitats. We believe that for such projects to be successful, they must have a carefully researched scientific basis and be carefully implemented and monitored.

The world is full of token service projects, those kind of works that make the doer feel better but do little to actually change the situation. Do not settle for those. Take the time to find real conservation work that can be done by you and your group of volunteers. But where do you look and what can be started on your own?

1. First, find and support vocational professionals in your congregation. Do you have men and women who worship with you who are

geologists? Hydrologists? Ornithologists or biologists? Do you have farmers? Gardeners or park rangers? Teach them to start with God in their own life of faith and help them integrate their faith with their practical work. When they are prepared, ask them to identify a local need in their field where you live and have them lead your congregation in action to make that one thing right. For example, A Rocha has Professor Mark McReynolds from Biola University on the national board of directors. Dr. Mark is an ornithologist, and any local project or local church would be foolish not to take advantage of him, his knowledge, and his connections. That church should be studying local birds, banding, researching migrations, or monitoring invasive species.

2. You can begin good works on your own if you desire. In Santa Margarita, we have helped develop the Creation Care Camp curriculum (see the appendix for more on Creation Care Camp) and have served hundreds of children and their families in our community over the last three years. Those families also gain a new connection with our congregation. Camp allows us to partner with many other organizations, as well, but more on that in a moment. In several locations, A Rocha-related projects and churches have planted community gardens. These gardens have taken on a different focus in each place. One garden was planted with the intent of selling the organic produce to local customers through a CSA (Community Supported Agriculture) program where families commit to purchase a box of seasonal produce each week of the growing season. This garden then began to sell the remainder at a local farmer's market. Another garden gives away the entirety of the produce to local food programs so that the needy have fresh vegetables along with their regular food distribution. Still another has used its garden as a way to bring families on to the property where they teach them to plant, care for, and harvest their own vegetables and teach them to cook them, as well. The opportunities in your place are endless if you have a little dirt and some time and volunteers. See the appendix for an excerpt from A Rocha's Garden Manual.

God's restored people restore people and places

Community

Through our commitment to God, each other, and the wider creation, we aim to develop good relationships both within the A Rocha family and in our local communities. A great deal of contemporary environmentalism sees human beings as most of the problem; we see them as part of the answer. Our reasoning is both theological and practical: theologically, we see human beings and communities as being important; practically, we believe that a conservation project is only likely to be successful when a local community comes to value it. As a result, we have a commitment to involvement with local people, whether in education or development projects. All A Rocha projects are focused on involvement in a community, often being based around a residential centre. Because we believe that community is so important, we aim to develop within our teams those principles of openness, honesty, and caring that are essential to healthy communities.

That place is your place; those people are yours. If I were wanting to start a new creation care restoration project where I live, I would first gather a community of like-minded Christians to talk, think, and pray about what God desires to be restored in our place. At A Rocha we take a "community first approach" rather than a project first approach. Build the relationships, pray together, learn together, dream together, plan together, and then implement that plan together.

1. Talk about your desire to see people and places put back together and find you might be interested, as well. Take advantage of church newsletters, social media, etc. to find those who are like-minded in your church and in your town.

2. Start with prayer when you gather for the first time. Praise God together for the gift of both your people and your place. Praise with as many specifics as you can. Confess where you have not loved people or place. Confess where you have felt superior to people, even in regards to your concern for creation, and have taken advantage of your place. Ask God to give you his heart for people and place, so that you may love them the way he loves them. Ask him to give you wisdom and vision. Ask God to give you the resources to accomplish that vision. Finally, give thanks to God for putting you in your place and for bringing this community together.

3. Choose a book to read as a community, tying the first two categories together. Maybe start with this book and go from there. Growing in our learning together also serves to bind us together because we are growing in the same direction. Meet regularly and allow the conversations to go in both personal and practical directions. Talk together about what you love about your people and your place. Talk together about what you see needs your love and attention. Do be careful not to become critical together; let your talk be redemptive. Being guided by a book can build community, as it allows an outside voice to speak truth with authority into your gathered group.

4. Invite a local professional to talk to your group about theological connections between you and your place. Invite professionals to speak to you about the uniqueness of your area so that you might be informed, inspired, and more connected to your place. A Rocha Nashville invited Robin Godfried from the Center for Religion and the Environment to address their group of songwriters before they broke up into groups to compose together. That weekend project resulted in the album *From the Smallest Seed*, which we call the soundtrack to the creation care movement.

5. Work or volunteer together doing something that you love. Like those songwriters who do what they love to do and are bringing benefit to every place where Christians are caring for creation, you can do what you love. Again in Nashville, many of the local project volunteers are mothers of small children. Jenna Henderson leads them to work together networking their backyards in restoration projects and that project has become the foundation of a nationwide effort. For both of these groups of people, community has built restoration, and the restoration efforts have built their community relationships. What is particularly genius about these folks is that their good work is closely tied to the lives that they already live; this is what we mean by creation care as whole life discipleship rather than a new program. See the appendix for information on the Backyard Habitat program.

6. Healthy communities are an essential part of healthy places. It takes effort to keep people and place together; make that effort. Do not allow the birds or the gardens to become more important than the people or even separate from the people. People slow you down, but it is a good thing to slow down.

God's restored people restore people and places

Cross-cultural

We draw on the insights and skills of people from diverse cultures, both locally and around the world. In a world of extraordinary environmental richness and varied human cultures, environmental problems are inevitably diverse. This diversity poses problems. Uniform solutions tend to be inadequate; what works in one place, may not work in another. It is also easy to overlook situations in one part of the world where solutions to problems have been developed that may be applicable elsewhere. A Rocha's rooting in the Christian church helps surmount these problems. Intellectually, being part of a body that extends across all cultures and languages gives us a prior commitment to cross-cultural relationships. Practically, our existing international links through churches give us immediate access to communities across the world that secular organizations do not have.

A Rocha is a unique organization because of our international quality. Biannual gatherings of A Rocha National Organization leaders allows cross-cultural cross-pollination where ideas, truths, and victories are shared for support and inspiration. Your local church may or may not have the same kind of international connections, but there are several ways in which the advantages of cross-cultural community can come to your local place.

1. Every local church has international missions; think both locally and globally in your ecological work as well. What work can you support internationally with your time, presence, and resources? What work can you support through your existing missionaries to see a greater restoration in the places their already work? Most missionary organizations already think this way. WorldVision supports water and sanitation, for instance. Our local church works with Amor Ministries, which builds houses for families in Tijuana, Mexico, where water and sanitation are big concerns. A Rocha got its start in an estuary outside of Lisbon because you cannot separate people and place. Destruction of that estuary would inevitably hurt local people. The protection of that estuary, a great value in its own right, has also served local people and brought the gospel clearly into the lives of many. A Rocha has grown over thirty years into Brazil, Bulgaria, Canada, the Czech Republic, Finland, France, Ghana, India, Kenya, Lebanon, the Netherlands, New Zealand, Peru, South Africa, Switzerland, Uganda, the UK, and the United States. Many, if not most, of these locations welcome both visitors and volunteers. Come and see what God is doing.

You Are There

Let it inspire you as to what might happen in your own place. See the appendix for more on A Rocha in the USA.

2. Think cross-culturally locally. If there is great diversity where you live, then gather with cross-cultural partners and do cross-cultural projects. Many churches provide ESL classes for immigrants to the area. Some have welcomed immigrants to the community gardens to show them what grows in their new homeland and sent them home with food and seed. Perhaps you can take a more radical step, as some are doing, and intentionally gather both volunteers and professionals from cross-cultural backgrounds so that you have a greater wisdom involved in your project and bring greater restoration to your people and place.

Cooperation

We work in partnership with a wide variety of organizations and individuals who share our concerns for a sustainable world. We seek cooperation with others for several reasons. Theologically, we follow the one who said "For even I, the Son of Man, came here not to be served but to serve others, and to give my life as a ransom for many." (Mark 10:45, NLT). Practically, active partnerships with those who are engaged in similar areas of work enable us to share resources, learn from one another, and achieve far more than we could in isolation. They also ensure accountability in all our work. In many cases, A Rocha's refusal to empire build has meant that we have been able to play a major role as mediators and intermediaries in the sometimes fractious world of environmental politics.

Chances are good that areas that need restoration where you live have already come to someone's attention. Who is doing it? How do you find out? How do you engage? Where do you find groups of people meeting together to do good in a place? Every community has them; you just have to know where to look. Here are a few places I have found helpful:

1. Go to your local library. Most libraries have a wall of community related groups or committees posted for publication. Look there, then go back again in a few weeks and then go back again. Ask the librarian, "Are there any groups that you know of who are serving the children of our school district? Cleaning up our creeks? Etc?" They just might know of someone.

2. Go to your school district offices. Districts often have volunteer committees that do good for the local schools. For several years I served on a committee that ran a drug-free community program for high school students every spring. If you think that this is not near enough to your mission, do it anyway. On that committee, I met several men and women, as well as the mayor, who changed my life, whose story I already told you. I made a great friend named John who worked in community outreach for the city and invited me to join in on other programs. Then I met the head of the local United Way and invited him to lunch. We spoke for awhile about all the good his program was doing; I commented that he didn't have any representation of the local churches on his board. He thought about it, realized I was right, and invited me to take part.

3. Go to the police department or sheriff's department. Go to the nearest Bureau of Land Management office. Look for Land Conservancy, Sierra Club, or 4-H. And, honestly, Facebook is an amazing place to find groups that are doing good in your area. Just search the name of your town and see all that brings up.

4. Go to your local farmer's market and ask questions of the farmers. Ask about their produce. They will love to tell you about it, but also ask about ways you can support or get involved. Are there local CSAs that you can join? Is there a community garden already going that you can just show up and join? In our area, several vineyards use their captured water runoff to plant vegetable patches that volunteers harvest for the local food bank. This is a great project.

5. Start your own Creation Care Camp and invite others to join you. In the first three years of this project, we have invited friends who are local professionals, but not part of our church, to teach our kids. We have had ranchers, farmers, and beekeepers. We have learned from a wildlife rescue, the Audubon Society, local park rangers, spinners, and water resource managers, just to name a few.

Go in and ask questions. Listen to the answers. Be willing to stick around and just serve: short-term good work is still good work. Partner with as many people as possible in as many ways as possible with the people you live with. Be a part of that community. This is worth church staff time; staff presence makes a difference in community organizations. Staff can then organize lay people to get involved and to lead where needed. Now conclude and act.

You are ready to take some practical steps as a church for tangible restoration of your people and your place. Write it down and get going. See the appendix for the A Rocha Project Manual for starting a more substantial conservation project in your area.

- What is the greatest need that you see? Dream about what that specific concern would look like in your place if it were substantially restored.
- What would get from here to there? Do you need more education? Will a study build both Christian understanding and community? Do you just need to get a shovel in the ground?
- How are you going to measure real practical results of your actions?
- Get going. Start small and enjoy. Be committed. This is a long project.

You are there

This book is not about *you*; it's about *us* as local churches. As a local church pastor, I believe that the local church should care about conservation because it (the church) is God's way of getting his people in the right place for the job. The church is where God uses the gospel of salvation in Jesus to restore people. God sends restored people to places that need restoration. God's restored people restore both people and places. This is what we mean by creation care.

You, church, are a local gathering of believers. You are a gathering of people defined by your faith in Jesus and the dirt you walk on. You are a people that always have a place. You are to be concerned with the real people and place to which you are sent. When you act locally, you act freely and with hope in the place you call home. When you act locally, you love your neighbors. When you love your neighbors, they are saved and restored. When they are restored, people and place are put back together.

Let me say this as simply as possible and leave you to it with all the blessing of God on your life and mission.

You: You are a divinely empowered Christian community, filled with the Spirit of God to do all of God's holy will. You have been saved from eternal death for your sins when God became a man in Jesus to die in your place. And you have been sent by that same Jesus, on a local mission, that

God's restored people restore people and places

includes both the people you live with and the place where you walk together. The two are never really separate.

Are: You are right now, at this time in human history, this moment that is different from all other moments, present in that place. You are verbally, actively, supernaturally, great-commissionally present. You are sovereignly present by God's deliberate design and for God's intended ends. Both the people and the place should flourish under your stewardship and all the more as you add steward disciples through your gospel community.

There: You are located in a particular place in the world that has a name, a history, and boundaries that are geographical, regional, sociological, and economical. You live among a people who share all of those particulars with you, and no other church in the world can say that. No other people are more capable of, more gifted to, and more prepared to bring all that God intends for that people and that place than you are right now.

You are God's people, at this time, in that place . . . and he desires to see the pieces broken by sin put back together by the grace of God through you. That is why it is good news that *you are there*.

Let's close this pastoral conversation with a benediction. Let us bow our heads together and pray the prayer of Basil the Great, an ancient prayer that flowed from the heart of a man of God nearly two millennia ago.

"The earth is the Lord's and the fullness thereof": O God, enlarge within us the sense of fellowship with all living things, even our brothers, the animals, to whom thou gavest the earth as their home in common with us. We remember with shame that in the past we have exercised the high dominion of man with ruthless cruelty so that the voice of the earth, which should have gone up to thee in song, has been a groan of pain. May we realize that they live, not for us alone, but for themselves and for Thee and that they love the sweetness of life.[1]

And all God's people said . . . Amen.

---

1. Quoted in Faw, *A Brief Theology of Creation Care*.

Appendix

Here are some resources available for your use from A Rocha (http://arocha.us/) to assist you in acting locally with freedom and hope in the place you call home.

Backyard Habitat Program. It is not enough to simply "care about" the creation and tick that box, we must actively *care for* it. What is needed is action that yields meaningful results, explicitly connects to faith, is easy to understand and implement, fits busy schedules, is family friendly, and glorifies God. This kit is meant to guide you towards making your own outdoor living space—whether a farm, a suburban lot, or the deck of a high-rise apartment—more friendly to the species that share and live in your area.

Why Every Church Should Plant a Garden and How. Whether in Genesis, Jeremiah, or the Gospels, gardens play a prominent role in God's plan. It even starts in one. A garden is a wondrous place where we can "meet" with the Lord and marvel at his miracles. It's a place to love your neighbor, care for creation, and grow veggies. No wonder churches everywhere are interested in them. They see them as a way to meet local needs. Some have planted food pantry gardens, giving the produce to food banks. Others rent plots on church grounds as a way to use the land productively and respond to a tight economy. Still others have reclaimed derelict inner city properties, transforming vacant lots. In the process, gardeners from these projects have enjoyed a greater sense of community, a joy in connecting with the natural world, and a healthier diet. All of which is good. But church gardens can be much more. They can meet needs and at the same time celebrate the bounty of God's good earth. A way to grow both food and community. A way to honor and care for people and for the planet. This easy-to-read manual is

Appendix

for churches, school,s and groups interested in growing gardens and blessings for their communities.

Creation Care Camp Curricula. Closely connected to *You Are There*, this vacation camp, suitable for grades 1–8, invites a sense of wonder and teaches children about creation and creator by combining God's word, science, and hands-on activities. Campers learn about the particulars of their place through exploring and discovering local plant and wildlife, habitats and water systems, while learning and applying biblical stewardship and discipleship to their interaction with the people and place around them.

A Rocha Project Guide. A booklet to guide any group wishing to start a conservation effort in their own community. Association with A Rocha can take several forms. Some efforts operate as A Rocha projects, others as independent A Rocha Affiliates, still others as simply friends serving a common cause. The vision is like that of Nehemiah: to help people build sections of the wall where they live and then connect those sections to something larger, something greater: an international movement of Christians actively participating in the care of God's creation. This booklet is written to help you take your care of creation out of the house and out of the church and into the streets, fields, and streams in your community—to seek its peace and prosperity, to be an agent of shalom to all God's creatures, to help you figure out what to do after you've changed the last light bulb.

And more resources are coming. Join us as together we build a movement of people caring for God's very good creation!

Bibliography

Berry, Wendell. *The Gift of Good Land*. San Francisco: North Point, 1981.

———. *What Are People For?* San Francisco: North Point, 1981.

Berry, Wendell, and Wes Jackson. "The Land, Our Food and Our Responsibility." *Convocation and Pastor's School: Our Daily Bread*. https://itunes.apple.com/us/itunes-u/2007-convocation-pastors-school/id420550036?mt=10. 2007.

Bock, Fred, ed. *Hymns for the Family of God*. Nashville: Paragon, 1976.

Carson, D. A. *The God Who Was There*. Grand Rapids: Baker, 2010.

Collins, Billy. *Nine Horses: Poems*. New York: Random House, 2003

Crouch, Andy. "The Joyful Environmentalists." *Christianity Today*, June 2011. http://www.christianitytoday.com/ct/2011/june/joyfulenvironment.html.

Damiani, Aaron. "Food is the New Sex." *Christianity Today*, April 2014. http://www.christianitytoday.com/parse/2014/april/food-is-new-sex-part-2.html.

Eberstadt, Mary. "Is Food the New Sex?" *Policy Review*, February and March 2009. http://www.hoover.org/research/food-new-sex.

Faw, Rick. "A Brief Theology of Creation Care." http://goodseedsunday.com/resources/theology-of-creation-care.pdf.

Harris, Peter. *A Rocha International Newsletter*. Issue 49, December 2010.

———. *Kingfisher's Fire: A Story of Hope for God's Earth*. Oxford: Monarch, 2008.

Kostamo, Leah. *Planted: A Story of Creation, Calling and Community*. Eugene, OR: Cascade, 2013.

Kunstler, James Howard. *The Geography of Nowhere: The Rise and Decline of America's Man-Made Landscape*. New York: Touchstone, 1993.

Lewis, C. S. *Present Concerns: A Compelling Collection of Timely, Journalistic Essays*. London: Fount, 1986.

Peterson, Eugene H. *Christ Plays in Ten Thousand Places*. Grand Rapids: Eerdmans, 2005.

Piper, John. *The Pleasures of God: Meditations on God's Delight in Being God*. Portland, OR: Multnomah, 1991.

Plath, Sylvia. *The Bell Jar*. New York: Cutchogue, 1971.

Pollan, Michael. *The Omnivore's Dilemma*. New York: Penguin, 2006.

Robinson, Tri. *Small Footprint, Big Handprint: How to Live Simply and Love Extravagantly*. Boise, ID, Ampelon, 2008.

Schaeffer, Francis A. *Pollution and the Death of Man: The Christian View of Ecology*. Wheaton, IL: Tyndale House, 1970.

Stott, John. *The Radical Disciple: Some Neglected Aspects of Our Calling*. Downers Grove, IL: InterVarsity, 2010.

Bibliography

Timmer, Dave. "Beyond the 'Green' Commandments." *Flourish Magazine*, February 2011. http://www.flourishonline.org/2011/02/beyond-the-"green"-commandments/.

Tripp, Paul David. *Instruments in the Redeemer's Hands: People in Need of Change Helping People in Need of Change*. Phillipsburg, NJ: P&R, 2002.

Wright, Christopher J. H. *The Mission of God: Unlocking the Bible's Grand Narrative*. Downers Grove, IL: InterVarsity, 2006.

www.ingramcontent.com/pod-product-compliance
Lightning Source LLC
Chambersburg PA
CBHW031503160426
43195CB00010BB/1086